Kissing The Mirror

Kissing The Mirror

Raising Humanity in the Twenty-first Century.

Mama Marlaine

BALBOA.
PRESS

A DIVISION OF HAY HOUSE

ISBN: 978-1-4525-5107-4 (sc)
ISBN: 978-1-4525-5105-0 (hc)
ISBN: 978-1-4525-5106-7 (e)

Balboa Press books may be ordered through booksellers or by contacting:

Balboa Press
A Division of Hay House
1663 Liberty Drive
Bloomington, IN 47403
www.balboapress.com
1-(877) 407-4847

Because of the dynamic nature of the Internet, any web addresses or links contained in this book may have changed since publication and may no longer be valid. The views expressed in this work are solely those of the author and do not necessarily reflect the views of the publisher, and the publisher hereby disclaims any responsibility for them.

The author of this book does not dispense medical advice or prescribe the use of any technique as a form of treatment for physical, emotional, or medical problems without the advice of a physician, either directly or indirectly. The intent of the author is only to offer information of a general nature to help you in your quest for emotional and spiritual well-being. In the event you use any of the information in this book for yourself, which is your constitutional right, the author and the publisher assume no responsibility for your actions.

Any people depicted in stock imagery provided by Thinkstock are models, and such images are being used for illustrative purposes only.
Certain stock imagery © Thinkstock.

Printed in the United States of America
Library of Congress Control Number: 2012909483

Balboa Press rev. date: 8/2/2012

In loving dedication to my mother
Ari Marie Evelyn Coulombe Sasanoff
Thank you for teaching me we are not our wounds,
we are not our weaknesses,
we are miracles,
each unique and
powerful beyond knowing.

In Gratitude

Thank you Billy, Ari and Alexa for surviving my steep learning curves,
making life joyous, and loving me always.

Thank you Michelle, Renee, Jami, BJ, Jesse
and all of your beautiful children for gracing my life journey.

Thank you Bill and Bob for fathering me.

Thank you Keyuri Joshi for your faith in me
and for unceasingly illuminating my path.

Thank you Melissa Pazen
for your prayers and unending love and support.

Thank you Tara Kennedy Kline and
Omar Benedir for sharing my vision of a Kinder Village.

Thank you Gloria Antonelli for being the wind beneath my wings.

Thank you Larry Wilcox and Neville Billimoria for your passion
and selflessness.

Thank you God for so graciously leading the way when I let go.

Thank you Parenting 2.0 for restoring my faith in humanity.

Contents

Foreward

I can't even remember exactly how we met - I just know it was one of those beautiful synchronistic happenings that make life a magical playground. From our very first introduction, I knew Marlaine was a "unique." A "unique" is someone who stands out in the crowd, regardless of what they're wearing, what color their hair is, or whether they are talking loud or whispering. A "unique" is someone whose passion is so clear, whose mission is so unshakeable, that you find yourself irresistibly drawn to them like an iron shaving to a magnet.

It was in the middle of our first or second phone conversation, when she mentioned she was editing *Kissing the Mirror,* that I blurted out, "I'll write your foreword if you want!" That's how pulled I felt into the magnetism that surrounds Marlaine – a magnetism I have since learned is nothing less than an international consciousness movement called Parenting 2.0. Founded by Marlaine in 2009, and inspired by her rejuvenating, home-spun, perspectives on how all of us can better flourish on this chaotic planet we call home, Parenting 2.0 is blazing new educational trails in countries around the globe.

Marlaine begins *Kissing the Mirror* by describing "The Mandatory Curriculum" facing every human being. She then affirms your personal ability to excel thanks to your "human GPS." Her introduction of The Life Skills Report Card, a communication tool she created out of desperation while raising her own two daughters, blends wisdom and whimsy while providing a dramatic paradigm shift for human development. The Life Skills Report Card is a system. System is an acronym for:

S-Save
Y-Your
S-Self
T-Time
E-Energy &
M-Money

As Marlaine writes "Free will does not mean you choose the curriculum. It merely permits you to choose the amount of suffering you and others endure until you learn a better way of doing things." My own life took an empowering turn when I first read her Life Skills Report Card. My initial thought was, "Damn, I wish I'd had that download previously! Powerful!" I then contemplated how such a simple concept could begin to positively change the world.

An excerpt from "*Kissing The Mirror*":
"A poem titled 'Children learn what they live' is internationally famous. Its popularity among educators and the families they serve is tragic. Why do people around the world readily support children spending decades learning math, sports, and music from third party credentialed instructors, but accept children's education in Life Skills as being limited to parents' behavior? What price do we pay for this impoverished narrative for human development?"

The Life Skills Report Card, however, is just one of many ideas Marlaine shares in *Kissing the Mirror* that will have you examining age-old assumptions in a new light and tackling tough child-rearing challenges with renewed confidence and vigor. In fact, if the book only contained Chapter 7 on Failure (which itself provides enough sanity wrapped in a big red bow to transform the whole of society) reading it would be one of the best investments of your life.

I've always said that the proof of a great writer is that in simply reading their words, an instant transformation within one's own psyche occurs. Prepare to be transported into a world where inner wisdom reigns supreme: A world where love, compassion, humor, humility, and enthusiasm for learning are an all-time reality. Prepare yourself for Parenting 2.0.

Janet Bray Attwood
NY Times Bestselling Author,
*The Passion Test – The Effortless Path
to Discovering Your Life Purpose*

Introduction

One Saturday morning, my husband and I returned home from shopping to find the first floor of our home covered with two inches of water. Although the process of mopping it up seemed simple, it actually took weeks for a team of professionals to dry out spaces between walls and replace carpets. All of this would have been wasted effort, however, had we not taken time to also identify and repair the source of the flood – a broken washing machine hose.

In every problem there is one critical point where the least amount of effort can yield the maximum results. For the flood in our home, that critical point was the washing machine hose. The water, while admittedly attention grabbing, was neither the source of the problem nor the solution.

The good news is that after the hose was repaired, and restorations were complete, our home was in better shape than before the flood. And so it is with our lives. Once we identify the real source of our difficulties, and focus our energies on repairing the hose instead of complaining or blaming others for the flood, things improve dramatically – seemingly miraculously. By contrast, if we never fix the hose and continue washing loads of clothing and mopping up floors, we qualify for the definition of insane.

Think for a moment about the last thing that troubled you. Did the same thing ever bother you previously, perhaps multiple times? If the answer is yes, rest assured it is because you were focusing on the water not the hose. Kissing the Mirror provides a new paradigm for examining the origin of your difficulties and achieving authentic correction.

Central to the discussion is the topic of Life Skills and the introduction of a communication tool called the Life Skills Report Card (LSRC). The LSRC defines Life Skills as, "all the non-academic, foundational skills we learn in our lives to thrive individually and commune optimally with others." Life Skills include, but are not limited to: Personal Care, Organizational, Safety, Management of Time and Finances, Communication, Social and Environmental.

Kissing the Mirror is divided into four sections, each is written to inspire thinking about your own educational journey with Life Skills and the benefits of embracing a more dynamic narrative for human development. Section one, "The Mandatory Curriculum", sheds light on the two assignments facing every individual – surviving and communing with others. It also advocates a measurement for success independent of academic achievement. Section two, Algebra and Apples, discusses weaknesses of academic principles for succeeding in The Mandatory Curriculum.

Section three, The Life Skills Report Card, takes Life Skills out of parental junk drawers and examines them as unique and distinct skill sets. It also introduces the concept of Life Skills Report Cards. Section four, The Change, describes the birth of an international volunteer organization, The Global Presence. The Global Presence provides a platform for "basically good people" to congregate and be the change the world awaits.

Section One
The Mandatory Curriculum

Chapter One
The Assignments

When you were born, you arrived hard-wired with two assignments. Nothing you have ever been – or will be – asked to do is of greater significance than these assignments. Consciously or unconsciously, you have worked on these assignments every day of your life, every hour, every minute – you work on them even when you are sleeping. You will continue to work on them every day until you die.

Your proficiency with these assignments determines your health and well being, the quality of your relationships with colleagues, friends, and family, the quality of your relationship with yourself, and whether or not you leave this planet a better place than when you arrived.

Do you know what they are?

You are not alone. Every individual has the same two assignments. Up until now, you may have underestimated the significance of these assignments. You may have undervalued the benefits of education and guidance from qualified teachers. You may even have been told you were ill-equipped for these assignments – or destined for failure. In private moments, you might believe there is something permanently wrong with you.

This is not true. You were born exceedingly well-equipped to excel with the two assignments you were given and, with proper education and encouragement, you will. Central to success is being aware of the assignments and having able teachers. Central to success is a willingness to be humble and welcome a picture of yourself larger than the one you presently envision.

Welcome to The Mandatory Curriculum

The First Assignment…

The first assignment in The Mandatory Curriculum is **to live.** That sounds simple enough doesn't it, a bit like permitting your heart to beat? Please pause a moment, however, and look at this assignment more closely. What does the low end of living, survival, entail? Who do you know that is surviving? What are their circumstances?

Now consider what the high end of living, thriving and living to your maximum potential, involves. Are you envisioning fancy cars, a mansion perhaps? Who do you know that is thriving? What are their circumstances? How do you define thriving?

On a sunny Seattle morning in March of 1992, I awoke to find my wrists and ankles bound in leather restraints and chained to a hospital bed. Ten months previously, I'd completed a Masters Degree program in Public Administration with a 4.0 GPA. Four weeks later, I gave birth to my second child – Alexa Marie – an exquisite, blue-eyed, auburn haired daughter.

As I tried recalling how I managed to end up thus confined, a nurse entered. "I cannot believe I left those scissors next to you!" She exclaimed as she picked up said hardware and rapidly left the room. "*What exactly did she think I was going to do?*" I wondered, "*Pick up the scissors with my mouth and stab myself to death?*" "*Yes,*" my conscience answered, "*that is precisely what she thought. What did you do, dear Marlaine, to inspire such thinking in another human being?*"

The first thing I remembered was a conversation with my youngest sister BJ. We were seated on the back porch of my brother's home. BJ was smoking and – although I was a non-smoker – I asked her for one too. After inhaling deeply, I told her I wanted my ashes spread over the Cascade Mountains.

Just one hour earlier, I'd laid Alexa in her crib for her afternoon nap and attempted to sleep also. BJ was visiting our sister Renee with my four-year-old daughter, Ari, and wasn't due home for two hours. My husband of six years and I had recently separated and we were living on opposite coastlines. Although I left him – desperate to shield our daughters from our ongoing arguments – I was deeply distraught and hadn't slept or eaten properly in weeks.

My mother was greatly concerned and took me to a doctor. He diagnosed me as depressed and put me on anti-depressants. Underestimating the depth of my condition, however, he neglected to educate me fully on the journey one takes when recovering from depression. He failed to inform me it is normal for some patients to feel suicidal in the process of recovering from severe depression, and what to do if I did.

I once heard suicide described as anger turned inward. Although I now think there are a million reasons people attempt suicide, and that physical health factors in far more significantly than commonly acknowledged or appreciated, that definition describes my experience well. Unable to sleep, I got up from the bed. Before reaching the bedroom door, I detonated. Without any forethought or reservations, I angrily began slamming through every cabinet in the house, taking all the pills I could locate. I might as well have been a bomb exploding.

Afterwards, an abnormal calm settled in. I sat down on a chair at the dining room table fully prepared to welcome whatever came next. The thought of writing a note to loved ones didn't even enter my mind. Then the unanticipated happened – BJ returned home. Fortunately she was alone.

BJ was my youngest sister and what little conscious mind I retained demanded I prepare her for what was about to transpire – so I told her what I had done. With great cool and collectivity, she called paramedics. By the time they got me to the hospital and pumped my stomach, however, it was too late. So they flushed me with fluids and my family prayed for my survival.

Developed countries, and increasingly underdeveloped countries, place an exceedingly high value on academic education. The general logic is this; the higher an individual's education, the higher the level of employment they will procure; the higher their level of employment, the higher their standard of living; the higher their standard of living, the greater their potential for thriving. Consequently, millions of children around the world spend the majority of their most formative years being educated in academics.

Let's imagine you have a high paying job in a field of your preference, and ample money to enjoy a high standard of living, what other things will contribute to you thriving? What about your health, your relationships, your thoughts? The fact is, you might have a high paying job and earn a great deal of money but if you do not prioritize taking care of your health and your stress levels you may not thrive. You may die a premature death.

What type of education have you received to strengthen your physical and emotional health? Who were your teachers? Have you completed nutrition and fitness classes? Have you ever attempted to strengthen your mental fitness? Have you ever even thought about mental conditioning? Are you able to maintain a clear mind for five minutes? Does it matter?

The Second Assignment…

The second assignment in The Mandatory Curriculum is to *commune with others*. This too sounds easy, right? Think for a moment what it means for you to be around others. How important is it? How important are relationships to you?

At the low end of communing with others we ignore, judge, abuse, torture, and kill one-another. Who do you know that is judging someone today? Who do you know that is killing someone? Why are they doing so? Who taught them how to get along with others? Who taught them communication and conflict resolution skills?

At the high end of communing with others we thrive personally and empower others to do the same. Who do you know that is thriving personally and empowering others? What skills enable them to do so? Was the way they learned those skills accidental or intentional, passive or proactive? Does it matter?

The phone in the hospital room rang jolting me back to the present moment. Despite my dire circumstances, I found it incredibly funny to have a phone ringing next to a bed where someone had their hands and feet bound. When the same nurse who'd chastised herself about the scissors re-entered and picked up the receiver – which in those days was still attached to a cord - then asked, "Would you like to speak to your sister?" I was simply grateful she didn't fear me strangling myself.

"Hello," I said, cradling the phone between cheek and shoulder. BJ took a long draw on her cigarette and exhaled before answering. "Thank God you didn't die," she finally said. "I forgot where you wanted those ashes spread."

The next day I was asked if I would like to spend a couple weeks in a mental hospital. Having failed at murdering myself, I decided to accept the invitation. Billy flew to Seattle and took our daughters back home with him to Pennsylvania. Ari returned to the pre-school she'd attended prior to me taking her to Seattle and Billy found a day sitter for Alexa.

A week into my stay in the hospital, I was delivered papers informing me that Billy was seeking custody of our daughters. I was also mandated to appear at a preliminary custody hearing in Philadelphia in five weeks. Billy and I had only recently moved to Pennsylvania from Virginia. We were still living in corporate housing when I left him. I had no friends or family there, no funds for a hotel, and I was prohibited from seeing our daughters until my court date.

Excruciating while it was being separated from my daughters, the singular positive was Billy had the opportunity to experience exactly what working full time and caring for two young daughters alone entailed. Despite doing his very best, Alexa lost four pounds and was diagnosed as "possible failure to thrive."

Weeks later, a subsequent daycare provider informed us that Alexa repeatedly chose to settle in her car seat rather than play around the room like a normal one year old. The sitter expressed concern that such behavior possibly meant the interim childcare giver Billy hired (after returning with the girls to Pennsylvania) had kept Alexa in her car seat for a large portion of the day. Regardless the reasons for her weight loss, the bottom line was this: I had not only failed at the assignment of thriving personally, I was failing miserably in my role of helping those most innocent and dependent upon me to thrive also.

Life Skills…

The skills that enable people to survive and commune with others are appropriately called Life Skills. Life Skills include but are not limited to: Personal Care, Time Management, Organizational, Respect for Self and Others, Communication and Social Skills.

In contrast to academics, which children may or may not learn depending on geography, gender, and economics, acquisition of Life Skills is mandatory. Every individual, be they a world leader or a knife wielding gang member, learns and utilizes some measure of Life Skills. The only things optional about Life Skills development are your appreciation for their value, the time you dedicate to learning them, and the individuals you engage as instructors.

Consider for a moment the last thing that troubled you: Was it your weight or appearance? Difficulty communicating with a work colleague or family member? Physical or financial health? Time management or organizational skills? If your answer is yes, you were challenged by Life Skills. Now think about how you learned these skills. Who were your teachers?

Parents, daycare providers, and relatives are typically your first and most influential Life Skills educators. How you eat, stand, play with others, and solve problems all are learned, initially, from them. Where did they learn Life Skills? From a nutritional college, mediation clinic, or spiritual retreat? Not usually… The bulk of their Life Skills were learned from their parents. If their parents stood tall, they stood tall; if their parents ate junk food, they ate junk food; if their parents screamed and yelled, they screamed and yelled. Ironically – despite an abundance of uniquely qualified educators – the Life Skills educational process more closely resembles genetic inheritance than academics.

A poem titled "Children Learn What They Live" is internationally famous. Its popularity among educators and the families they serve is tragic. Why do people around the world readily support children spending decades learning math, sports, and music from third party credentialed instructors, but accept children's education in Life Skills as being limited to parents' behavior? What price do we pay for this impoverished narrative for human development?

> **Immediate Opening:**
> **Most Important Job on Earth -**
> **Raising tomorrow's leaders!**
> **No prior education, training, or**
> **experience necessary.**

If the first great irony in life is that the most important and widely shared job on earth – parenthood – has yet to merit any standard formal preparation, the second greatest irony is that we accept the Life Skills our parents teach us as if we were computer clones. Even if we hated the quality of Life Skills learned – barring some major personal crisis that requires us to examine their inferiority – we typically do very little to assess our abilities and continue our education as adults.

As a society we wholly condone formal adult training for everything from tattooing to mountain climbing. When it comes to the critical tasks of marriage and childrearing, however, the majority of people simply wing it. If difficulties arise family members attend "therapy."

Webster's defines therapy as "remedial treatment." Remedial comes from remedy, which means to "restore to health." Therapy, therefore, is a term that describes restoring someone to a state they were previously. If an athlete breaks their leg, they attend "therapy" to *regain* mobility. If someone suffers a stroke they attend "therapy" to *regain* their cognitive and motor skills.

How many individuals attending therapy to improve communication and relationship skills previously had what anyone would term highly competent ones? How can someone regain something they have yet to learn? Relegating education of communication skills to the confines of a doctor's office typically causes people to feel shame and embarrassment when attending class; this doesn't exactly create pride in the enrollment process. Does learning more effective ways to thrive in relationships really need to be any different than learning any other skill? Why do we wait for a crisis to learn something that can prevent it?

Think for a moment how critical interpersonal communication skills are in your life. Did you ever have formal education from third party instructors? Children are taught to read, write, and spell, but how many are ever taught active listening or conflict mediation? How might the world change if they were?

I obtained my undergraduate degree in communications and not one class provided instruction on interpersonal communication skills. The only place people received that type of education was when studying to work in mental health, legal, or enforcement fields (psychiatry, social work, law, therapy, the military etc.) In other words, we routinely prepare people to respond to crises in Life Skills but we do not prepare all people to excel. Why?

> *We routinely prepare people to respond to crisis in Life Skills but we do not prepare all people to excel. Why?*

Problems in our personal lives become problems in society. Take a moment and consider today's media headlines. What do you find? Stories about bullying and wars; local and global financial crisis; environmental decay? Inferior Life Skills have their roots in personal problems and, not coincidentally, societal ones. Examine any news headline and ask yourself, what skills are necessary for avoiding or resolving the problem? Then ask yourself, where do people learn these skills? Who are their educators?

State of the Union 2011: Lawmakers Cross Aisle, Sit Together, Make History

Bipartisan Seating Plan Yields Unusual Bedfellows in Show of Civility, Unity

BY DEVIN DWYER WASHINGTON, Jan. 25, 2011 ABC news

Yes, you read this headline correctly. Lawmakers of differing perspectives – governing one of the most powerful nations in the world – made international headlines in 2011 simply by sitting next to each other for the first time in 100 years. Is it really so surprising that if sitting next to each other took 100 years for some of the world's most sophisticated leaders, we have trouble with more complicated issues?

People in developed countries are more likely to spend hundreds of dollars on their hair and nails, or even thousands on new cars or plastic surgery, than they are to further their education in communication and conflict resolution skills. While it is popular to blame media for today's difficulties, the truth is the problems exist first.

Independent of every other headline topping newspapers around the world daily, I think the one above serves as a clarion call for us to reassess our appreciation for our Mandatory Curriculum and embrace a more proactive Life Skills educational process.

Lesson #1
Every human being faces the same Mandatory Curriculum -
surviving and communing with others.

Chapter Two
Curriculum Scholars

Knowing the low and high bars of achievement is critical to competency in any area. Life Skills are no exception. In contrast to academics, where the top level of performance is marked by 4.0's and individual success, the high bar in The Mandatory Curriculum is thriving personally and supporting others in thriving as well.

Many Curriculum Scholars are widely known and admired: Mahatma Gandhi, Mother Teresa and Nelson Mandela to name a few. The majority, however, are not publicly recognized for their contributions. Their names do not appear on plaques in tall glass towers or churches. They are not bestowed awards before hundreds or featured on the evening news and in magazines. Curriculum Scholars are loved by those surrounding them – in homes, classrooms, companies large and small, hospitals, slums, prisons, and orphanages.

Curriculum Scholars exist wherever there are human beings. They derive wisdom and strength from their own challenging journeys and inspire others to reach their maximum potential. Imbued with humility and compassion, Curriculum Scholars feel a sense of oneness with others and rejoice in their achievements.

The low end of performance in the Mandatory Curriculum is marked by thoughts of scarcity and fear – often veiled with a spirit of superiority. Individuals struggling with the Mandatory Curriculum view themselves as victims or heroes. They disparage, abuse, torture and kill others. Adolf Hitler, Benito Mussolini, and Joseph Kony are some of the more notorious strugglers.

Lesson #2
The high bar for performance in The Mandatory Curriculum is thriving personally and helping others to thrive as well.

Chapter Three
Torch Bearers

Talk show hosts and parenting professionals frequently excuse teens' behavior because of parents' actions. This is not a valid comparison. It is, in fact, like having a race to London with one person starting in California and the other in China. Life is not so much a one shot chance at the same basket as it is the Olympic Torch Run. Each generation – each individual – faces their own unique terrain and challenges. Personal strengths, weaknesses, and the choices children, teens, and adults independently make dozens of times daily, factor enormously into the equation.

> *"Discipline has changed since I was a kid. When my children do something wrong, my wife and I give them a "time out." Whenever I did something wrong as a kid my dad would take "time out" of his busy day to tan my hide." - Jeff Foxworthy*

Today's babies are expected to live past 80– 62 years as adults! That is a lot of time to improve upon parents' teachings. Where you start children on the road to life is just that, a start. Tell them this.

Tell them you improved upon your parents' parenting and you have complete faith they will improve upon theirs. Reassure them that they will have many teachers in their life, you are but one.

Instead of bemoaning their teen years when they are confident they know better, gift them a blank journal and encourage them to take notes while their thoughts are fresh. Then sit back and compliment yourself for a job well done.

Lesson #3
***Life is like an Olympic Torch Run with each generation,
each individual,
facing their own unique terrain and challenges.***

Chapter Four
Baby, You Were Born This Way

Please take a moment now and point to yourself. Where are you pointing? To your head? No, you are pointing to your heart. Why? Because that is where your human GPS, your hard-wired global positioning system, is located. Whether you call it your inner voice or God within, or fail to acknowledge it entirely, your human GPS knows what you need to thrive and commune optimally with others. Every living thing on earth has a GPS.

Like the heart that beats in your chest, your GPS is constantly giving you feedback, every second, every minute, every hour, every day. When your thoughts or actions do not facilitate you thriving and communing optimally with others, or a lesson before you is beyond your skill level, your human GPS sends off alarms. When it does, you feel fearful, upset, disturbed – even angry. When you ignore your GPS long enough, you can become physically ill or dis-eased.

Picture yourself driving to New York from Florida. You enter Times Square, New York, as the destination on your mobile GPS. Unfortunately, you end up talking to your passenger and miss the exit. In no uncertain terms, your electronic GPS instructs you to turn around. *Please note, your GPS does not instruct you to tell New York City to move, it tells you to change direction.*

Your human GPS functions the same way. It tells you when you are thinking or steering off course. In the same manner you experience peace when trusting and following your mobile GPS, so too do you experience peace when trusting and listening to your human GPS.

Whenever you are focused on what someone else needs to do, or how another person needs to behave in order for you to be happy, you are not listening to your GPS. You are attempting to reprogram theirs – you are instructing New York to move. That is your EGO (short for "Easing Guidance Out") functioning.

Brace yourself. Efforts to reprogram someone else's GPS will, at best, leave you in spin cycle, going around and around and never arriving at a satisfactory destination. At worst, someone will die. Even when your brain is too stubborn to listen, your GPS is still functioning. Have you ever asked your mobile GPS for instructions and then decided you knew better how to get somewhere? How did that work out for you? While you may feel temporarily better overriding your human GPS, you can prepare for that thrill to be short lived as well.

In the six years I spent obtaining college degrees the most valuable thing I learned, by a galaxy, was from a sociology professor who stated plainly one day, "Should is shit." For the next month, (well truthfully decade) I paid attention to every time I said or thought the word should. "The driver *should* have been more courteous." "My sister *should* have been kinder." "The sun *should* have shined today." Talk about living in the land of make believe!

Picture two race cars at the starting line: The flag drops and one driver hits the gas pedal. The other driver sits and complains how he *should* have had the other lane, how his mechanics *should* have finished their repairs quicker, etc. etc. Who wins? Life is the same. Should is the equivalent of the "Wrong Way" sign when listening to your own GPS.

Does this mean it isn't helpful to tell someone if they are on the right path when travelling to New York? No, every human being benefits from affirmation and encouragement. It simply means it isn't terribly helpful if you spend thirty minutes telling them all the reasons they are not on the right path – or them telling you.

Like the radar box in the movie *Black Hawk Down*, your GPS is always functioning within your heart, always waiting to guide and deliver you peace. Regardless the number of times you steer off course, your GPS is ever-present.

Listening to your GPS does not mean you won't suffer loss or pain; change is a part of life. People die, jobs end, houses burn down. It does, however, guarantee you will experience less pain and more joy irrespective your life experiences.

> *"Security is mostly a superstition. It does not exist in nature, nor do the children of men as a whole experience it. Avoiding danger is no safer in the long run than outright exposure."*
> *-Helen Keller*

How do you know when you are hearing your GPS? Think for a moment about something that pleases you. How does that feel? That is your body responding to your GPS. Now think about something that makes you angry. How does that feel? That is your body responding to your GPS also.

In the first situation you are thinking in alignment with your GPS, doing so brings you peace. In the second you are thinking out of alignment with your GPS, doing so causes imbalance – upset. Regardless of your life circumstances, you are **never** more than one thought away from being in alignment with your GPS.

Once again, peace of mind does not come from reaching New York; it comes from knowing you are on the right path when travelling there. Peace of mind is always available in the present, you experience it when you think and behave in alignment with your GPS.

The majority of the pain and upset you experience in your life does not come from actual experience. It comes from the pain you deliver yourself when you fight an experience, judge yourself or others harshly, or choose to relive a painful experience over and over again. Negative thoughts about yourself and others are the equivalent of drinking poison due to the stress hormones that flood your body when you embrace them. The hard truth is, you are your own worst enemy. The good news is you can begin today being your own best friend.

When you were born your brain was like a planet without roads. Every new experience activated a construction site, with neuron-sized workers moving dirt, pouring cement, and building new pathways. As a toddler you already had a vast network of highways. Repeating activities created freeways.

Children raised in high stress environs often have freeways to survival. The slightest stimulus can send their bodies into fight or flight mode, and activate hormones that facilitate fast defensive or aggressive actions. Saying something feels "easy" or "natural" does not mean you are in alignment, it simply means a freeway exists in your brain for that activity.

If you are thriving and others around you are thriving also, stay your course. If you are not, you can change. First, however, you must own your role as a construction worker. You must have a goal and be willing to work towards it. You must be willing to try something new - something that may initially feel discomforting.

Do you remember when you first learned to drive? It was intimidating – maybe even a bit terrifying. It required instruction

21

from someone who knew the rules of the road and demanded every ounce of your attention. In time, however, you learned you could reach desired destinations without conscious thinking. What power, what freedom!

You still can. You do so multiple times daily. In fact more than half of your actions each day are guided by your subconscious. Thank goodness! Otherwise you would be too tired from deciding which leg to move when walking, or how to deliver food to your mouth, to construct new roads.

Child-rearing literature frequently says what happens to you as a child will determine what you do as an adult. This is only true if you deny your capacity to construct new roads and permit your subconscious to continuously travel old ones. Regardless of your age, or the roads to hell you may have travelled in your past, you are always capable of thinking in alignment with your GPS and constructing new freeways to better destinations.

> *"The more man meditates upon good thoughts,*
> *the better will be his world and the world at large."*
> *-Confucius*

People often confuse not verbally expressing a negative thought with not thinking it. Once again, the road is yours. If you think it you construct it. While you cannot keep negative thoughts about yourself and others from surfacing – indeed they have roots in your subconscious and sprout without effort like the breaths you exhale – you have the power to choose whether or not you give them a seven course meal with candle light and friends.

In the same way construction workers have plans for minimizing consequences of bad weather or break downs in equipment, so too will you benefit by having a plan for dealing with things that negatively impact your road construction.

Several techniques exist - Transcendental Meditation, Tapping, and prayer to name a few. Only you can determine which work best for you. So commit to researching and experimenting. If you have never previously invested in your mental conditioning, prepare to be blown away by the richness of your real estate.

> *"The inner life is like a garden we haven't really thought of planting, which will bear all the fruit we could ever want once we think to tend its needs."*
> *— Marianne Williamson*

People used to believe that practicing positive thinking was nothing more than painting a moldy fence white. Modern science confirms that the opposite is true. Positive thinking brings light to the mold, and literally heals you from the inside out. Your relationships, mood, and appearance will all soon reflect that which you have chosen to treasure. Ill thoughts of others primarily hurt you. Believing otherwise is to accept one of the greatest lies ever promulgated by the human race.

> *"Those who blame others, suffer much."*
> *-The Dalai Lama*

People often think, "If I just quit this job; if I just leave this spouse, I will be at peace." But then they quit the job, leave the spouse, and they are not at peace. Why? A road to peace cannot be constructed with judgmental thinking – it can only be constructed with thoughts of peace. Your GPS knows this. The sooner you take care to listen to your GPS, and stop condemning past behavior of yourself and others, the sooner you will thrive. Like any skill, listening to your GPS improves with commitment, time, and practice.

Want to do a quality control check on your construction site? Place ten pennies in the center of your desk or kitchen counter. Each time you catch yourself having a loving, compassionate thought about yourself or others move one penny to the right. For every judgmental thought move one penny to the left. Do this for one week to get a more accurate sense of your performance.

Then stop counting your negative thoughts and simply add a penny to your stockpile for the positive ones. Know that every penny you add is an investment in construction of new mental freeways to paradise – freeways you will travel on every hour, every day, every year, for the rest of your life. When your thoughts change, your life changes, invest in yourself. Don't measure your improvement by anyone else's standards, only your own. Your GPS will be the first to smile upon you and provide you a standing ovation.

Lesson #4
Your human GPS
is your personal compass for thriving.

Chapter Five
Mandatory Matters

People often point to daily news stories as evidence of humans' natural desire to dominate and harm others. If this were true, news of violence would not be newsworthy. Violence is news because the stories are not commonplace. Human beings are herd mammals, hard-wired to care for others. They know there is strength in working together. If someone else is suffering it is a sign they may soon suffer also.

Picture yourself in a nursery. Would you ever point to one of the babies and say that baby was bad? Would you say one of the babies was born to be violent? No, with only rare exceptions in neurological development, violence is a learned response – it comes when we ignore and live in opposition to our GPS, not as a consequence of it.

Newborns are very clear about their hardwiring. When they are distressed or hungry they cry; they don't attempt to tough it out or adorn false smiles. When one infant cries in a nursery, others cry in empathy.

> *"Love is what we are born with. Fear is what we learn here. The spiritual journey is the relinquishment – or unlearning – of fear and the acceptance of love back into our hearts."*
> *-Marianne Williamson*

In my early adult years I was attending a community college on Capital Hill in Seattle and living in an apartment building across the street. One Friday afternoon, I left my apartment to deliver a paper to one of my instructors. As I was crossing the street, a man about 6' 8" and packing easily 300 lbs. of muscle approached the school's entrance as well. Although he was not wearing military clothing, and didn't display any unusual mannerisms, the second I saw him my internal GPS registered him as someone who'd been through extreme trauma, a Vietnam Vet perhaps.

"Do you go to school here?" he asked as I reached for the handle. "No, I'm just dropping something off to a friend," I lied; simultaneously realizing the door was locked. "Do you?" I asked, looking him squarely in the eyes. "Yes," he replied as he pulled on the opposite door – which also turned out to be locked. The same GPS that told me he'd suffered trauma told me he was lying. It also told me he knew the same about me.

"Staff must have left early for the holiday weekend," I said shrugging my shoulders and turning back to the entrance of my apartment. "Yeah, I forgot it was a holiday," he said as he mirrored my turn and slowed his gait to match mine. He feigned calm. I knew I was in trouble. Unfortunately, my options were limited. With the college closed there were neither cars nor people on the street and, given his size, there was definitely no way I could outrun him to the nearest open place of business. So I decided to continue to play it cool and permitted him to enter the main entrance of the apartment complex with me without asking further questions.

Our apartment building was nine stories tall, with the main entrance located in the center of the first floor. I lived on the second floor and always took the stairs, situated just inside the main entrance, rather than the elevator. As we strode together toward the staircase, he walking to my left and the elevator to my right, I casually said,

"Well, have a great evening," then reached out and punched the up button, turning my back to him.

Thankfully, he continued up the staircase. The elevator doors opened and I exhaled deeply as I entered. My brain raced through possible escape options. I decided he would not likely think I would use the elevator to travel just one floor and also calculated that with his long legs he could climb a couple floors quickly. So I took another deep breath, pressed the number two and got off, praying he was at least a floor above me. My apartment was located on the far end of the hallway to the right. I immediately saw that the path was clear, but I looked left just to make sure.

There he stood, at the end of the hallway, back flattened against the sidewall, the frame of his body hidden in the shadows of the hallway light. He knew exactly where I lived and he was positioned to attack. The second I saw him my body exploded into survival mode. I wheeled around and raced down the stairs, knowing I had but seconds to find safety. The manager's apartment was on the main floor and I hurled towards their front door like a boulder, grabbing the handle but fully prepared to break through if necessary.

As it happened, the door was unlocked and I nearly knocked over their teenage boy as I entered. "A man is chasing me," I explained in hurried breath as I closed the door behind me. No sooner had I uttered the words than I saw the 4" straight, blonde hair that topped my stalker's head passing the manager's apartment windows. "That's him," I said, enormously relieved to see him leaving the premises.

While it may have seemed natural to call the police, absent any real physical harm or contact, I decided against it. I did, however, move in with my parents for a few days. For some reason the man's energy refused to leave my system. I felt toxic, as if poisoned. My stepfather insisted I call the police.

"But Dad," I protested, "He didn't actually harm me, what on earth can they do?" After three days my stepdad simply dialed 9-1-1 and handed me the phone. Within fifteen minutes, a plain clothed police officer was seated with me in our living room.

I explained to him what had happened and how shocked I was by the effect the man's energy had on my body. Rather than minimizing my concerns, the officer leaned forward empathetically and said, "I have been responding to these types of calls for years and every single time, without exception, the women sensed danger before something transpired."

He then added, "Normally we do not divulge information about ongoing investigations, but two weeks ago a young woman was raped and bludgeoned to death in the laundry room of an apartment complex a few miles from yours. We found four inch straight blonde hair at the scene and we know, from the force with which he struck her, that he was exceedingly strong."

I share this story not to condemn the man who stalked me, precisely the opposite. I share it to underscore the significance of the mandatory assignment of communing with others. Many people take great pride in their independence. The fact of the matter is, however, independence is an illusion.

We are seven billion people living interdependently in a finite space. Even if you elect to live all by yourself in the pristine wilderness of the Yukon Territory, if someone sabotages a nuclear plant in California you may die. Failure to care for the child three blocks from you may result in you working to pay taxes to keep her in jail ten years from now.

> *"Even more important than the warmth and affection we receive is the warmth and affection we give. It is by giving warmth and affection, by having a genuine sense of concern for others - in other words through compassion - that we gain the conditions for genuine happiness."*
> –The Dalai Lama

Every adult has a role in raising future generations. With children as young as six being arrested and hauled off in handcuffs from elementary schools for "bad behavior" the question you must ask is, "What can I do differently?"

Lessons #5
Free will does not mean you choose the assignments. It merely permits you to choose the amount of pain you and others endure until you learn what is necessary to thrive and commune optimally with others.

The Mandatory Curriculum Lesson Summary

Lesson #1
Every human being faces the same mandatory curriculum:
surviving and communing with others.

Lesson #2
The high bar for performance in The Mandatory Curriculum is
thriving personally and helping others to thrive equally.

Lesson #3
Life is like an Olympic Torch Run with each generation,
each individual, facing their own unique terrain and
challenges.

Lesson #4
Your human GPS is your personal compass for thriving
and supporting others in thriving also.

Lessons # 5
Free will does not mean you choose the assignments. It
merely permits you to choose the amount of pain you and
others endure until you learn what is necessary to thrive and
commune optimally with others.

Section Two
Algebra and Apples

Chapter Six
Heart Surgery with a Chainsaw

I am the second of five girls and my biological father was an artistic type who played the piano by ear, painted, and ice-skated. He also worked two jobs to provide food and shelter for his children. Consequently, we didn't have very much in the way of Home Depot tools around the house. If we needed to hang a painting or repair a cabinet, my mother would typically grab a shoe (wooden clogs were fortunately vogue in the seventies) and hammer away.

Absent a more appropriate tool one uses what's available, right? So it is understandable that lacking proper education in interpersonal communication and social skills, "educated" people use the terminology learned in academics to relate to others and resolve conflicts.

Unfortunately, while the wooden clog might be an acceptable substitute for a hammer, utilization of academic principles like Right/Wrong, Perfect/Imperfect, Smart/Stupid, when our goals are thriving personally and communing optimally with others, is a bit like performing heart surgery with a chainsaw.

Have you ever argued about something, swearing your opinion was "right" and the other person's opinion, by necessity, "wrong"? Did you become highly emotional in the process as if being called "wrong" was somehow life threatening?

In academics, there is typically one correct answer. Students are rewarded for knowing this answer and penalized for alternate perspectives. In The Mandatory Curriculum, far more frequently than not, there are multiple right answers – multiple perspectives and opinions – each entirely valid.

Consider for a moment a grocery market. Ten people enter, ten people exit, each with something different. Does the fact that one person purchased bananas and another person bought apples make either of them right or wrong? If nine people buy bananas, and one person buys apples, does that make the apple lover bad?

On any given day, life is like a great big market, with thousands of things attracting your attention. In your exchanges with others – whether at home, work or socializing – you are but a shopper in the grocery store. You can pay attention to what pleases or what displeases. What you focus on always communicates far more about you, your personal preferences and sensitivities, than what is in the market.

> *"An old Cherokee told his grandson. 'My son there is a battle between two wolves inside us all. One is evil. It's anger, jealousy, greed, resentment, inferiority, lies and ego. The other is good. It's joy, peace, love, hope, humility, kindness and truth.'*
> *The boy thought about it and asked 'Grandfather, which wolf wins?' The old man quietly replied, 'The one you feed.'"*
> - Cherokee Proverb

Paying attention to what displeases you rather than what pleases you constructs a freeway to displeasure in your brain. Continue doing so and you will soon travel there regularly without conscious effort. This is the reason some people earn the reputation of being "chronic complainers." They are, and they work daily repaving the road to ensure they remain miserable.

While you may be brilliant pointing out what something is *not* in a math class, it is often considerably more boring when it comes to general observations, comparable to saying an orange couch is *not* brown. Thanks to years of academic conditioning, however, a surprising amount of human interaction is spent describing the oh so fascinating, entirely exhilarating, miraculously stimulating, infinitely intoxicating land of *not*-ness.

"The teacher is *not* kind." "The dress is *not* pretty." "My father is *not* cool." Attention to what many things are *not* comes at enormous expense of seeing and nurturing things that are beautiful and valuable.

When I was a little girl my mother told me a story about six blind men, an elephant, and a wise man. The wise man asked each blind man to stand around different sides of the elephant and tell him what type of animal stood before them. One man, touching the elephant's tusk, described it as smooth, cool and sharp. A second man, holding the elephant's ear, described it as rough and flat. And so they continued. The wise man then told them, "You are all right."

If you only surround yourself with people that see life the same way as you, people you deem as "worthy," you will miss the elephant's toes and their relationship to its tusks. You will miss the majesty, diversity, and divine interconnectedness of the miraculous world before you.

Lesson #6
Personal perception is necessarily
subjective and limited.
Retire being "right," respect perspectives of others.

Chapter Seven
Failure

Failure, while much derided in academics, is essential to success in The Mandatory Curriculum. Failure builds humility, compassion for others' struggles, and confidence in the rewards of persevering through difficulties and disappointments – essential attributes for inspiring the same in fellow human beings.

Whether learning to walk on feet for the first time, or circumnavigating the globe in a sailboat, success in the Mandatory Curriculum demands trying new things, it demands risks. Consequently, it also entails multiple missteps and often even very public upsets. As P.J McClure brilliantly stated, "If you want to join the Success Club, failure is the cover charge." Consider for a moment the individual whose famous name precedes the following resume:

Failed in business	1831
Defeated for legislature	1832
Failed in business again	1833
Elected to legislature	1834
Nervous breakdown	1836
Defeated for speaker	1838
Defeated for land officer	1843

Defeated for congress	1843
Elected to congress	1846
Defeated for re-election	1848
Defeated for senate	1855
Defeated for vice president	1856
Defeated for senate	1858
Elected President	1860

The Answer? Abraham Lincoln. The official White House website provides the following biographical details about one of the United States' most beloved and revered Presidents.

"Abraham Lincoln (February 12, 1809 – April 1, 1865) served as the 16th President of the United States from March 1861 until his assassination in April 1, 1865. The son of a Kentucky frontiersman, Lincoln had to struggle for a living and for learning. Five months before receiving his party's nomination for President, he sketched his life: *"I was born Feb. 12, 1809, in Hardin County, Kentucky. My parents were both born in Virginia, of undistinguished families--second families, perhaps I should say. My mother, who died in my tenth year, was of a family of the name of Hanks... My father ... removed from Kentucky to ... Indiana, in my eighth year... It was a wild region, with many bears and other wild animals still in the woods. There I grew up... Of course when I came of age I did not know much. Still somehow, I could read, write, and cipher... but that was all."*

As President, Lincoln built the Republican Party into a strong national organization. Further, he rallied most of the northern Democrats to the Union cause. On January 1, 1863, he issued the Emancipation Proclamation that declared forever free slaves within the Confederacy.

Lincoln never let the world forget that the Civil War involved an even larger issue. This he stated most movingly in dedicating the military cemetery at Gettysburg: "*we here highly resolve that these dead shall not have died in vain--that this nation, under God, shall have a new birth of freedom--and that government of the people, by the people, for the people, shall not perish from the earth.*'"

Modern technology and social media have made instantaneous global connections for human beings possible for the first time in human history. Everyday citizens are now able to communicate with millions. This worldwide democratization of power and influence is miraculous. With the same technology able to broadcast individuals' every failing also globally in seconds, it can be tempting for today's young people to avoid taking risks.

> *"The fearful are caught as often as the bold."*
> *-Helen Keller*

In The Mandatory Curriculum, those who take risks and fail learn humility and compassion, essential skills for becoming a Curriculum Scholar.

Lesson #7
Those who take risks and fail learn humility and compassion, essential skills for becoming a Curriculum Scholar.

Chapter Eight
Difficult

Parents and children readily accept that school will be difficult. If a child finds a particular subject harder than others, parents know that reducing student to instructor ratio and intensifying practice time will facilitate learning. The concept of "difficult" when considered in the lens of academia simply means challenging. We do not call the child difficult because they are facing a difficult assignment, we call the *assignment* difficult.

When it comes to the education of Life Skills, however, (personal care, organizational, interpersonal communication and social) we call the *child* "difficult", or some other name: "messy, lazy, rude, selfish, bully, victim, drama queen, shy, fat, crybaby, dumb." Educated adults create bigger names: "obstinate, ignorant, arrogant, intolerant, belligerent, self-aggrandizing."

Rather than increasing instructors and supporting students faced with difficult assignments, as we do with math and reading, we label, berate and punish. Instead of appreciating one another as learning, we pass moral judgments and condemn others for their struggles. Why?

> *"Freedom is not worth having if it does not connote freedom to err."-Mahatma Gandhi*

How might children and adults' performance with Life Skills improve if we better acknowledge the learning curve and take greater care to support all persons in the totality of their education? What options exist for doing so?

Some parents elect to home school their children in order to separate them from the "negative influence" of other learners. While academic instruction delivered at home may prepare children to adequately meet academic standards, the Mandatory Curriculum provides considerably more rigorous challenges. Public school is not simply about academics or spoon-fed social lessons. It is a rich laboratory for Life Skills education – a microcosm of the larger world.

Whether dealing with difficulties communicating with a teacher, responding to pressure or abuse from peers, or simply being exposed to human beings whose home lives and values differ vastly from your own, public schools provide thousands of opportunities for learning to thrive as compassionate, contributing adults in an imperfect, diverse, and often contentious world. By acknowledging the significance of these opportunities, and providing proactive instruction and guidance, you can empower children rather than limit their education.

Lesson #8
Like academics, Life Skills benefit from
proactive education, qualified instructors
and a dynamic curriculum.

Chapter Nine
Graduation

While children in developing countries strive to build and attend primary schools, and females battle for the same access to academic instruction as males, children in developed countries often count the days to the end of the 13 year reign when they will be free of academic imprisonment – unless of course they attend college, in which case they have a few more years to suffer.

Unfortunately, graduation, whether from high school or college, typically marks the beginning of the hardest phase of learning for the Mandatory Curriculum: marriage, employment, children, financial challenges, local and global governance, all lie ahead.

What other position on the planet involves ceasing preparation and education at the very same time a task monumentally increases in difficulty? Far from being the time to stop learning, young adulthood is when human beings – and the societies they shape – benefit most from continued education by qualified instructors.

Lesson #9
The harder the task,
the greater the value of instruction,
at any point in life.

Chapter Ten
Learning

Billy won custody of the girls when I returned to Pennsylvania for the preliminary court hearing. His attorney, however, told him I would very likely be awarded custody in the actual hearing. So we decided to sit down together and work out our own terms of separation. We agreed to formally separate for one year and each attend therapy. We also decided the girls would reside primarily with me, since Billy was the primary bread earner.

One of the most valuable lessons I learned during our year of separation was the power of my foundational beliefs. If I believed I was destined to thrive, I found evidence to support it. If I believed I was broken and forever wounded, I found evidence to support that.

Another was learning the difference between codependent and unconditional love. Codependent love is being kind and expecting kindness in return, then punishing others when they fail to return the kindness. Unconditional love involves giving freely without conditions. Unconditional love is not given in anticipation of compensation. The reward is received in the emotion of loving and the expression of gratitude through giving.

Prior to Billy's and my separation, I believed that if I was sufficiently "good" and "loving" all would be well. The truth, however, is that I was not loving; I was conditionally loving. When

Billy did not behave in a manner I considered appropriate I judged and insulted him. I ignored my GPS and our relationship predictably deteriorated – as did my relationship with myself.

When we reunited we committed to appreciating ourselves as "learning" and accepted the fact that failure would be a natural, indeed necessary, part of the process. We also forgave one another when we did something poorly. This enabled us to move from constant judgment to encouraging one another when we did things well. None of this happened overnight, but we had a goal of making it work and we were willing to be patient with our learning curve.

As I write this I am in my upstairs office and I hear my husband grunting downstairs:

"What are you doing?" I ask.

"Cleaning up mustard I spilled on the white carpet," he responds.

"How's it going?"

"Well, it's not a total failure. The sponge is getting yellow. But we may have to buy a new carpet."

Suffice to say, at age 59, with a Ph.D. in Biochemistry and a J.D., Billy is still learning – as am I. Ironically, we discovered interpersonal communication skills benefit from the same educational principles and processes as golf (which Billy loves):

1. Perceiving the skills as valuable.
2. Desiring to play even when conditions are less than perfect.
3. Having confidence that practice over time leads to better outcomes.
4. Appreciating mistakes as a natural part of learning - and knowing everyone has unique strengths and weaknesses.

5. Embracing instruction from third party educators optimistic about our ability to excel.
6. Commitment to practicing for "years."
7. Complimenting one another for things done well.
8. Taking mistakes lightly.
9. Enjoying the journey.
10. Knowing that beginners are no less valuable of human beings than experts.

One of the biggest limitations to many "Healthy Family" cookbooks is that they promote one "correct" way of being and behaving, rather than valuing various stages of the Life Skills educational journey equally. This is comparable to applauding tenth graders and disparaging second graders.

A second is that by advocating a "correct" way of being, they breed intolerance for diversity. Why do humans treasure rarity in everything from fish and birds to flora but when it comes to people they deem as "different" they label them "abnormal"?

I have an extended family member, age 45, who has a low IQ. Several months ago we were discussing a woman who was cruel to her during an interview. I told her, if we had a test that measured kindness, she would score higher than the woman who was cruel. She liked that quite a lot.

We can be aware of averages, of things that are common and things that are rare, but who is qualified to define normal? Even those supposedly charged with the task can't agree. Just this week, March 19th, 2012, Time Magazine ran an article about a scientific storm brewing around the revisions to one of the medical profession's key diagnostic manuals, the DSM (short for the Diagnostic and Statistical Manual of Mental Disorders.) It reads, "First published in 1952, the DSM attempts to catalog every psychological problem human beings experience. The new edition set to be published next year will be the first revision since 2000. It will literally redefine what's normal."

Billy and I were keenly aware our functioning was a far cry from Dr. Phil's definition of a "Perfect Family," but it was our life, our baby steps to applaud, and our new story to invest in improving. We also knew that just as diversity was beautiful in plants, so too was it beautiful in human beings.

In the same manner gold is surrounded by dirt, qualities you love in others often surrounded by qualities you dislike. Gold is dirt before it becomes gold. Knowing this, and hanging in there for the gold rather than throwing the relationship away due to annoyance with the dirt, delivers real-life human treasure – emotional, physical, and spiritual.

Lesson #10
You can walk away from a person
but you cannot walk away from the assignment.

Algebra and Apples Lesson Summary

Lesson #6
Personal perception is necessarily subjective and limited.
Retire being "right," respect perspectives of others.

Lesson #7
Those who fail learn humility and compassion -
essential skills for becoming a Curriculum Scholar.

Lesson #8
Like academics, Life Skills benefit from
proactive education and a dynamic curriculum.

Lesson #9
The harder the task,
the greater the value of instruction from qualified educators,
at any point in life.

Lesson #10
You can walk away from a person
but you cannot walk away from the assignment.

Section Three
The Life Skills Report Card

Chapter Eleven
The Life Skills Report Card

"You may be getting an A in European History but you are flunking personal care 101!" I hollered after Ari (age 14) as she ran out the front door for school one morning without eating breakfast. Was it any wonder? She had a mad woman wearing a bathrobe screaming at her for an Educator.

The silver lining of failing at tasks others deem simple is you gain a fresh perspective on ordinary things. Sometimes you are even inspired to improve upon existing processes. So it was with me and Life Skills. Having experienced first-hand the deterioration in mental functioning that occurs when we fail to properly care for our human bodies, I took far greater effort to better nurture mine after Billy and I reunited. Sleep, exercise, and spirit all became far higher priorities in my life.

When they did, seemingly everything in my life improved. Life was not perfect, far from it, hence my hollering at my daughter. Being perfect, however, was no longer a goal - learning was. Having gained much insight from my own difficult journey, I had a deeper personal appreciation for the instructional value of failure and the satisfaction of small improvements.

By paying attention to the way certain actions delivered predictable results, I began to choose and behave differently. For example, instead of automatically feeling attacked if my husband hollered, I learned I could choose to see him as overwhelmed. When I did, and responded in a reassuring manner rather than attacking back, he calmed. When I chose to argue back, well….that's why they are called "fights."

Having the "power to choose" did not mean I always "chose" the peaceful path. Sometimes I enjoyed - and even initiated - an argument. Sometimes I still do. But the awareness that I had greater personal power to determine the outcome of a situation - that I was in fact responsible for the quality of my relationships with others - was empowering beyond description.

Billy's and my crash course in interpersonal communication skills greatly influenced the way we raised our daughters. Whereas fellow parents labeled girls "drama queens" when they came home complaining about conflicts with friends, we affirmed for our daughters the fact that emotional intelligence was as – if not more – critical for their success in life than academics. We also assured them few things would deliver a greater return on investment than learning to view theirs and others learning curves with appreciation and compassion.

We were also (me I confess more so) passionate about the girls' sleep routines and diet. Even well into their high school years, we firmly enforced the rule of no electronics – only reading – after 8pm, and very often they were asleep by 9pm. In addition to requiring they turn all electronics off by 8pm, we insisted they have breakfast before leaving for school each morning. One day, however, Ari was running late. Instead of taking one moment to drink her protein drink, she exited the front door screaming, "I don't have time."

After hollering back at her (as previously confessed) and slamming the front door, I resumed housework and committed to feeling sorry for myself. Fueling my lament was the realization that

I was vastly outmanned in my role as a Life Skills Educator – and my daughters knew it.

For academics they had mandatory attendance, credentialed instructors, and a standardized curriculum. For Life Skills education, by contrast, they had family life and friends - and a society that held fast to the concept that children simply "learned what they lived." While it was common for parents to invest years and hundreds - even thousands - of dollars ensuring their children excelled in math or music, when it came to learning how to keep personal items organized they were simply expected to "obey" - and punished or disparaged when they "disobeyed."

I knew that if I was not part of the solution I was part of the problem. Since report cards were routinely appreciated and accepted in academics, I decided a similar format would be valuable for communicating with my daughters regarding their Life Skills. So I sat down and created the Life Skills Report Card.

I divided critical Life Skills into the following categories: Personal Care, Organizational, Respect for Self and Others, Communication and Social. Subcategories included Sleep, Safety, Time Utilization, Finances, Altruism and Environmental Consciousness.

That weekend I made the girls their favorite breakfast of French toast and bacon and proudly introduced my new communication tool. I asked them to grade themselves first, then I provided my review, and we discussed where we saw things differently. This alone inspired much laughter.

Next, we chose one area to strive for improvement and mutually contributed to solutions. I also agreed to let their performance in other Life Skill areas – temporarily - slide.

To be honest, I was enormously humbled realizing how many things my daughters were in fact "learning" on top of academics. I was also embarrassed by the manner I had been demanding (rather than inspiring) peak performance. Not surprisingly, they too found the entire process infinitely preferable to mom screaming at them.

Following is an abbreviated copy of our Life Skills Report Card. You can download a complimentary copy of the full version (which has more space for comments) at http://parenting2pt0.org. Please note that, just as academic report cards vary for different ages, values and cultures, so too will Life Skills Report Cards. I share ours merely as a concept and encourage you to personalize.

No one, of course - neither parents nor children - needs another thing to do at the end of the day. Since education of Life Skills is something you are dealing with everyday anyway, often in reactive rather than proactive means, the Life Skills Report Card will serve as a time saver rather than a time stealer.

Regardless the subtopics you assign to each category, I encourage you to retain the quantity (six), corresponding numerical values and Total Life Skills Average (maximum possible points is 150). As with multiplication tables, learning new ways of doing things takes commitment to practice over weeks. For this reason, I recommend reviewing Life Skills Report Cards on a schedule similar to academic report cards.

The Steps to Success section provides room for itemizing key things you agree to focus on in the upcoming quarter. The Progress Notes section is provided for recording progress you make between your review sessions. "Out of sight out of mind" most assuredly applies so, rather than placing the LSRC in a drawer when you're finished, tape it instead in a quasi-private location such as the inside door of your child's closet or a kitchen cabinet. This will keep your goals visible. Critical while it is to be patient and permit learning to develop over time, if something proves to clearly not be working, be humble enough to sit down and discuss an alternate strategy for success.

LIFE SKILLS REPORT CARD©

Personal Care	Low – High
Sleep	1 2 3 4 5
Food & Water	1 2 3 4 5
Exercise	1 2 3 4 5
Spirit	1 2 3 4 5
Safety	1 2 3 4 5
Appearance	1 2 3 4 5

Organizational	Low – High
Clothes	1 2 3 4 5
School	1 2 3 4 5
Sports	1 2 3 4 5
Other	1 2 3 4 5
Time utilization	1 2 3 4 5
General schedule	1 2 3 4 5

Respect for Self and Others

Bedroom and household maintenance	Low – High
Household rules	1 2 3 4 5
Property of self and others	1 2 3 4 5
Transition times	1 2 3 4 5
Manners	1 2 3 4 5
Finances	1 2 3 4 5

Progress Notes:

_____

_____

_____

Communication	Low – High
Use of "I" statements	1 2 3 4 5
Proactive/Assertive	1 2 3 4 5
Creativity/Humor	1 2 3 4 5
Solution oriented	1 2 3 4 5
Listening/Feedback	1 2 3 4 5
Appropriate vocabulary	1 2 3 4 5

Social	Low – High
Avoids criticisms/ Focuses on positives	1 2 3 4 5
Takes ownership in problems and conflicts	1 2 3 4 5
Shoots for win/win outcomes	1 2 3 4 5
Shares/Altruism	1 2 3 4 5
Enjoys variety of activities	1 2 3 4 5
Environmentally conscientious	1 2 3 4 5

Total LSA
(Life Skills Average) _____

Steps to Success:

_____

_____

_____

In the next few chapters I discuss the five individual categories of the Life Skills Report Card: Personal Care, Organizational, Respect for Self and Others, Communication and Social. I also share personal stories to inspire reflections on your own educational journey with Life Skills.

I believe we all grow softer and wiser when we read stories that underscore our shared humanness so, please keep a pen handy when you read. In future editions of *Kissing the Mirror*, I would like to feature your stories.

> *"We judge each other so quickly, yet know so little about what another carries in his or her heart. To truly awaken to grace and sacred presence we must offer to all the same respect we would give a great teacher."-Jack Kornfield*

Humorous stories and videos are particularly welcome. Videos will be featured on our Life Skills Report Card channel on YouTube. You can submit both via the comment section on the Parenting 2.0 website: http://parenting2pt0.org

Lesson #11
If you are not part of the solution,
You are part of the problem.

Chapter Twelve
Personal Care

Just as performing algebra is possible only when you have first mastered addition and subtraction, so too is success with communication and social skills dependent upon mastery in the areas of personal care - hence the priority placement of Personal Care on The Life Skills Report Card.

Sleep, Diet, Exercise: It is common knowledge that when children are tired or hungry, working through life's challenges - academic or personal - is difficult. When they are well rested and fed, it is significantly easier. Yet how often do parents permit children to stay up late watching TV and then go to school the next day tired? How many children skip breakfast or fail to drink eight glasses of water daily?

One day, my daughter Alexa returned home from elementary school exhausted, hungry, and complaining about difficulties she was having with her best friend Amanda. Rather than speaking directly to her conflict with Amanda, I gave her a hug and said I was sorry she'd had a challenging day. I then asked if she wanted to take a bubble bath with candlelight while I heated her up some soup. Alexa's shoulders relaxed immediately and she flashed me an appreciative smile.

After soaking in the bath and eating her soup, she curled up on the couch where I was reading and started talking about Amanda again; this time her tone and perspective were considerably more thoughtful.

"Mom, you know when I was taking the bubble bath," she said, *"there was this one bubble that I really wanted to pop, but every time I tried to pop it would just pop up elsewhere." "So then I started to get angry and I slammed the bubble with my full hand. You know what happened?"*

"You flooded the floor?" I asked with mocked dread.

"No," she replied indignantly, "I got a hundred more bubbles, but then guess what I did?"

"Splashed even harder?" I asked feigning even greater dread.

"No, I just laid back and did nothing and guess what happened?"

"What?"

"The bubbles popped all by themselves. I just needed to be more patient. That's what I think I need to be with Amanda," she concluded.

When gardeners want a rose bush to bloom they do not instruct it, they provide it adequate water and soil. Children are not terribly different. Their innate brilliance blossoms when you take care to prioritize foundational personal care needs first and give them quiet space to listen to their own GPS.

Sadly, adults today are often more likely to prioritize gas and oil for their autos than water and sleep for children. It is estimated that more than half of all headaches have dehydration as their origin – not lack of aspirin. Adults are often not any better with themselves. Type II diabetes - wholly preventable with proper diet and exercise - causes more deaths than breast cancer and AIDS combined. It is predicted to affect one of three US citizens by the year 2050. (ogs. cnn.com/2011/06/24/five-diabetes-myths-busted/).

Daniel Amen, a psychiatrist and author of *Change your Brain Change your Life*, is one of today's leading advocates of healthy living as it relates to daily functioning and relationships. In his efforts to help people work through their problems, Dr. Amen began scanning brains. In so doing he learned a very simple fact - healthy brains reflect themselves in healthy lives. The reverse is also true, healthy lives reflect themselves in healthy brains. It was no coincidence that my suicide attempt came after weeks of intense stress and difficulty sleeping and eating – in fact it was nearly predictable. Adequate sleep, a nutritious diet, and regular exercise all contribute to having a healthy brain and body. These, in turn, positively impact every aspect of your life.

Spirit: Just beneath Sleep, Diet and Exercise, under the category of Personal Care, is Spirit. Many equate the word spirit with "religion" or "beliefs," I use the word spirit on the Life Skills Report Card to describe energy. When functioning at your energetic best you are "inspired" or experiencing a state of "flow." When you have spent your energy at a rate that outpaced renewal, you describe yourself as "drained," or "dispirited."

In the same manner the electrical grids for a building automatically shut down when demand exceeds supply, so too does your human body shut down. Depression is not your body malfunctioning, depression is your body protecting you from spending energy you do not have. Depression has the nickname "the dark night of the soul" because it is asking you to pay attention to the insufficient flow of "light" in your life.

Just as you would be foolish to leave your car lights on night after night and jumpstart your car each morning, so too are you foolish to jumpstart your body when it is depressed without also identifying why it became drained in the first place. Learning to maintain a healthy, energetic balance is a critical skill and one too little acknowledged or appreciated.

Absent severe genetic birth defects or irreversible damage due to physical injury, every human being is capable of being the vessel through which energy is flowing in abundance. Being honest about your present abilities, and finding appropriate teachers to enhance your techniques, improves performance. Learning new ways of inspiring yourself can be a life-altering gift for yourself and others.

Appearance: For better or worse we are primarily a sighted society. Most of us are more likely to hand our child over to a well-dressed stranger in a crisis than to someone who hadn't bathed in a week (even though the first person might very well be a pedophile and the latter a Saint).

As a child born with hopelessly straight blonde hair following the height of the Shirley Temple mania - to a mother blessed with an abundance of thick black curls - I spent many nights enduring hard plastic rollers in attempts to look like something other than a homeless child.

Even all the dolls manufactured and advertised at the time had curly hair - with the exception of one, Little Miss No-Name. True to her namelessness, she wore a patched burlap dress and was bare foot. A large plastic tear permanently adorned her cheek. Her straight, blonde, hair was cut unevenly at the shoulders completing her orphaned appearance. Today my daughters take straightening irons to their lusciously wavy locks!

Torture sessions aside, the fact is appearances matter. How we stand, groom, smile etc. communicates appreciation for ourselves and respect for the sensitivities of others. Given the discrepancy between the definition of beautiful hair when I was 10 and my own daughters at the same age, however, is it any wonder that we have different definitions for proper appearance when our children head out the door for school?

Rather than attempting to convince children you have the perfect solution for their "appropriate" appearance, embrace humility and mutually explore what is currently acceptable in various social circles. In the same manner children need to do their own math to learn, so too must they be permitted to err when it comes to appearance. Be willing to compromise and also permit them to fail.

When my nephew Bryce turned eleven, I took him shopping for new blue jeans. He was an avid skateboarder and wanted pants he could wear low on his hips like other California skaters. Having daughters, I wasn't familiar with boys' sizing charts, so I let Bryce pick out jeans he liked and try them on in the dressing room. Just three minutes after entering, Bryce came out holding the new jeans and beaming. I was thrilled our shopping had been so simple.

When we returned home my sister Renee (Bryce's mother) asked him to try them on. Two minutes later, Bryce came down the stairs wearing – or I should say barely managing to hold up - a pair of pants that could easily have swallowed two of him. Despite efforts to restrain ourselves, Renee and I dissolved into uncontrollable laughter and tears. Even Bryce conceded he overshot "baggy".

Safety: Completing the foundational category of Personal Care on the Life Skills Report Card is safety. Any adult who has ever been around a toddler knows that they are constantly trying to off themselves by chewing on electrical cords, hurling themselves down flights of stairs, or jumping into pools absent ability to swim. By the time my youngest daughter was five, however, I began to believe I was finally beyond the stage of constantly worrying about my children's impending funerals.

Wrong. One day, when I was working as a group tour planner and spending the morning at my travel office, I left Alexa and Ari at home with friends visiting from Germany. I'd known this couple for years. They are exceptional individuals and parents with two sons who were – at that time - teenagers and a daughter a year younger than Alexa. So I gave our usual sitter the day off and permitted my daughters to spend the morning with them.

A couple of hours after arriving at my office I received a phone call saying Alexa was "missing". "Oh, she is probably just hiding under one of the beds", I attempted to reassure them, "she plays that game often with her sister." "We've checked the entire house," they stated in an anxious tone. This time I took the information very seriously.

After talking among themselves, they determined that the last one to see Alexa was their teenage son Dominik. Alexa had followed Dominik into the front yard to watch him skate, then remained outside when he came back in. Learning this I became basically frozen with fear. "Call the police," I said, "and then call me when they locate her." My office was twenty minutes from home and in those days I didn't own a cell phone. While it may have seemed logical for me to return home and assist them in their search, I refused to believe Alexa would not be located within that extensive length of time. So I remained, instead, glued to the desk in my office waiting for the phone to ring.

An excruciatingly long hour later it did, with the information that volunteers had knocked on every door in the neighborhood and Alexa still had not been discovered. While I knew this fact greatly increased the likelihood that Alexa had been abducted, my mind refused to permit me to embrace the emotionalism of it. Too panicked to drive anyway, I continued to sit frozen at my office and said simply, "Keep looking."

Fortunately the police were way ahead of me, talking to volunteers and recording detailed information about each home contacted. One of the volunteers reported that he'd avoided knocking on one of the assigned residences, as he knew the couple worked during the day and their cars were gone as usual. "Go back and knock on the door anyway," the officer instructed.

Low and behold, a teenager answered the door. Behind her stood two little girls, one of them was Alexa. It turned out the teen's family also happened to be visiting from out of town. She'd taken her younger sister for a walk and on their way back they'd encountered Alexa. The younger girl invited Alexa to come play Barbies with her and the teen naively took her without notifying any adults. "Why did you go with a stranger?" I implored when I was tearfully reunited with Alexa again. "She told me her name mommy," Alexa replied simply.

That experience caused me to be far more cautious with my children than the average parent. Whereas thousands of children were permitted to ride their bicycles unescorted around their neighborhood daily, mine were not. Today's parents fortunately have several new technologies at their disposal. One example is Rescuehood, a mobile phone app that enables parents to broadcast alerts when their child goes missing. Created by Canadian software expert Randall Isaac, the alert is received by other mobile phones in the local area. Rescuehood rallies a community of instant responders who can help return the child to the parent before the situation becomes critical.

Another critical safety concern for children – one that dominated news headlines in the US recently with the conviction of Penn State University Football Coach Jerry Sandusky – is molestation. Oprah Winfrey, herself a victim, courageously educated millions via her daytime talk show of the fact that over ninety percent of all childhood molestations are committed by a friend or family member.

Schools regularly teach children to stop, drop and roll in the event their clothes catch fire but the reality is children are far more likely to be molested by someone they love. On one of her final shows, Oprah featured a district attorney and child safety expert named Jill Starishevsky. Jill wrote a beautifully illustrated book titled, *My Body Belongs To Me* to assist parents in teaching their young children how to protect themselves against child molesters. Precisely because parents routinely prefer to avoid this topic - believing it will never happen to their child - I recommend every family with toddlers add Jill's book to their child safety toolbox.

Teenage years of course bring a whole new array of concerns regarding safety. When our daughter Ari was learning to drive, we decided she – and the general public – would be safer if her first car was a truck. From Ari's response when we told her, you'd have thought we'd said her that her first car would be the trash collection vehicle.

To soften her upset, I reminded her of all the cute, girlish decorations she could use to decorate it – things like neon flowers and bumper stickers that said "Silly boys, trucks are for girls." That seemed to work. Once Ari actually had her own truck, however, I experienced an instantaneous 180 degree shift in consciousness. Suddenly such blatantly youthful, feminine auto advertisements seemed to translate to something along the lines of "Teenage Virgin, Easy Target". "How about we put up a bumper sticker that says 'Proud Pistol Packing Member of the NRA' instead?" I asked. We settled on nothing.

I wish I could say fears of my daughters being abducted were unwarranted. Tragically, 14 year-old Amber Dubois – a freshman attending Escondido High School where my daughter Alexa was a senior, was kidnapped while walking to school on February 13th, 2009. Freckle faced and innocent, she was carrying valentines for friends and a check for 4H in her backpack at the time of her abduction.

It took over a year and the murder of a second teen, beautiful, blonde 17 year-old Chelsea King jogging at a nearby lake, before the psychologically ill man responsible for both their abductions was arrested and the details of their deaths fully revealed.

Lesson #12
Respect personal care for its
foundational importance in every aspect of life.

Chapter Thirteen
Organizational Skills

Under the second Life Skills' Category, Organizational, are the following subtopics: Clothes, School, Sports, Other, Time utilization, and General schedule. Seat 30 parents in a room and 25 will tell you that children's lack of preparedness for school or sports ranks as a major source of conflict. Why? Because the parents never learned to teach effective time management or organizational skills so they make lousy instructors.

Clothes, School, Sports: Keeping track of necessary supplies does not come naturally to the majority of children. It is in fact a skill - one that benefits measurably by identifying precisely where difficulties exist when things are calm and committing to small steps for improvement. Unfortunately, parents frequently confuse children's struggles with learning organizational skills with misbehaving. They then lecture and punish instead of finding more creative ways to inspire pursuit of mastery.

In my early professional years I worked as a fundraiser for universities. The positions required simultaneous tracking of multiple minor details. Fortunately, I was introduced to a time management system called The Franklin Planner (now called Franklin Covey). The Franklin Covey system promotes abandoning post it notes and scrap paper and keeping information in one central planner. It also advocates spending fifteen minutes each morning and evening prioritizing activities utilizing the letters ABC - A activities being imperative, C ones that can be completed at a later date. The Franklin Covey system is so effective I still use it thirty years later.

As my children entered elementary school, I was pleased to see planners becoming a regular part of many schools' academic curriculums. In my later role as director of an academic tutoring club, however, I observed parents interfering in their children's learning curves with daily planners in one of two ways: They either under-estimated the value of developing mastery with the planners or they over-assisted their children in the learning process. These same dynamics frequently repeat with other organizational skills.

By choosing the area where your children are most motivated to achieve improvement (be it clothes, school or sports) and accessing wisdom of third party educators to support them in acquiring organizational mastery, you can use this success to inspire their confidence for succeeding in the other areas. The key is to dialogue with your children at pre-scheduled hours – not when they are rushing out the door to school or exhausted after returning home.

Be prepared, however, in the same manner you may be a poor fit for tutoring your child in math, so too may you be ill-suited for educating your child in organizational skills. Rather than paying therapists to deal with your child's "bad behavior," commit to keeping the educational process stimulating. Take time to simply talk about the learning curve with your child and access the wisdom of organizational experts like Mitzi Weinman or Wendy Joy Hart. By acknowledging you may have a few things to learn yourself - and incorporating others' ideas - you set a great example for life-long learning.

Time Utilization, General Schedule: One popular discussion among Life Skills Educators is how children spend their non-academic hours. Two concerns are commonly expressed: One is children being overbooked and overstressed – whereby they construct mental freeways to stress rather than joy. The other is children spending too much time with electronics, thus limiting their development of interpersonal communication and social skills. While each child is different, excess of anything typically hinders healthy growth. So take care to promote and inspire balance, while at the same time respecting children's unique personality and temperament.

Lesson #13
Just as you accept others teaching your children academics,
so too can others be more effective educators of Life Skills.

Chapter Fourteen
Respect for Self and Others

The third Category on the Life Skills Report Card is Respect for Self and Others. Subtopics include: Bedroom and Household Maintenance, Household rules, Property of self and others, Transition times, Manners & Finance.

Modern parenting professionals routinely cite the importance of earning versus demanding children's respect. What they too frequently fail to acknowledge, however, is that respect is often earned by others demanding it. Teachers, law enforcement, and coaches are examples of individuals that demonstrate personal respect for rules and policies by creating physical consequences for violations. In this framework, demanding respect earns respect.

Parents have an obligation and a responsibility to ensure the safety of their children. If they fail in this role, they can end up in jail. This responsibility gives them the "right" to demand respect. By providing consequences for disrespect, parents communicate their own respect for their rules. Whether children like the mandates or not is irrelevant, "Because I said so," is just as appropriate when employed by parents as it is by law enforcement.

This fact acknowledged, as with organizational skills, it is critical parents take care not to minimize the learning curves in the arena of communicating respect for self and others with simple mandates or punishments.

Bedroom and Household Maintenance: If the show Family Feud polled their audience for the top five aggravations of parents, bedroom maintenance would most assuredly be included. My eldest daughter Ari is so naturally organized she arranges the clothing in her closet according to style, sleeve length, and color shade. In fact, at the age of thirteen she forbade me from hanging up clothes in her closet because I lacked "sufficient intelligence."

By contrast, I once contemplated calling FEMA (The Federal Emergency Management Agency) due to the devastation caused by my youngest, "Typhoon" Alexa. (Yes, I too previously engaged in name-calling – I still do on occasion, particularly when other drivers are rude, but I am improving!) Just as some children need more creative techniques to master math or reading, so too will some require a more dynamic curriculum to master home maintenance.

Tempted while parents often are to close children's doors and ignore the disaster – indeed many do precisely that - this is no more appropriate than over-functioning and cleaning everything for them. Children need to ***learn*** that leaving baggies with half-eaten peanut butter sandwiches under their beds attracts insects and rodents. They need to learn that respecting the property of others is communicated by real action. Rather than simply mandating performance, however, make an effort to turn up the fun factor by playing their favorite music and joining them in the process. Teach by example that work can be enjoyable – not simply the legal definition of community service.

Life Skills we fail to learn as children carry over into adulthood. Billy and I were the textbook "odd couple." He is the third of four boys and happened to be raised with the assistance of a maid. I, second of five girls, was the maid. During our first year of marriage we were both working at Washington State University (WSU). Billy was a post-doctoral scholar in the biochemistry department and I was a capital campaign coordinator for the WSU Alumni Office. The hours we spent at home were limited and fairly comparable. Nevertheless, in a very brief time, I found I was doing most of the housework and greatly resenting Billy's inferior participation.

In complaining to my mother over breakfast one morning that the women's liberation movement accomplished nothing other than ensuring women "do it all," she introduced me to a book titled *No Trespassing* by Cornelius and Marianne Bakker (1973). No Trespassing discusses the problems that arise when we claim a territory larger than we can personally manage. It also says, to paraphrase, should we find it necessary to permit part of our territory to be managed by another, we need to let go of the expectation that it be managed exactly as we would manage it personally - less we earn the reputation of tyrant, nag, or worse.

The fact of the matter was I'd laid claim to a territory larger than I had time to manage – our whole house. To compensate, I attempted to instruct Billy's GPS and he of course rebelled. By over-functioning, I was also encouraging Billy to under-function. So, the first thing I did was sit down with him and work out a mutually agreed upon division of labor - not incredibly difficult since our rental house had all of four rooms; living room, bedroom, kitchen and bath.

The painful part was letting go of my desire to have an overall orderly house. I finally decided a clean kitchen and bedroom were absolutely essential to my sanity and chose those two rooms as "my territory." Billy acknowledged he trashed the living room and bath more than I did and took responsibility for maintaining those areas.

Most importantly, I made a personal pledge not to say anything to Billy about his territories. Fortunately, he was so horrible at his tasks that the challenge soon became pitiful enough to be hysterical.

Newspapers and dirty socks rapidly piled up in the living room - and I won't even begin to discuss the state of the bathroom. When showering and brushing my teeth, I simply pretended to be living in a developing country and embraced the opportunity to be grateful for sanitary water.

More than once Billy came home to find my girlfriends and I curled up in our bedroom on our neatly made bed drinking tea (out of pristinely clean cups) because the living room had grown uninhabitable. Eventually, even Billy grew tired of not having clean socks or being able to find mail amidst the newspapers. One day, miracle of miracles, I came home to find - not only the living room clean but - Billy on his hands and knees wearing safety glasses and gloves scrubbing the bathroom floor. I told him he never looked sexier.

Household Rules: Most parenting books advocate the importance of consistency in enforcement of Household Rules. In reality, however, one parent often ends up assuming the role of "the enforcer" while the other parent enjoys the role of the "nice parent or rule breaker."

From day one, of course, babies know mother and father are different – the same fact applies for same gender parents. One has a high voice, one has a lower one. One parent gets excited easily, the other less so. Parents are different and children know it.

Billy and I were sufficiently different to not even attempt convincing our children otherwise – even when it came to Household Rules. Instead of feigning a unified front, we used House Rules to teach our daughters that different people had different sensitivities and rules. If they went to their father for something, they would likely get one type of response. If they went to their mother for something they would get another. Mom bought granola, Dad bought Fruity Pebbles. Mom said things once then moved to action, Dad hollered five times then forgot he was upset. When my teenage nephew moved in with us for a few months the girls took care to inform him, "Beware, Daddy has the bark, but Mommy has the bite."

We did, however, tell the girls that if they went to their father first for something his response would stick. If they came to me for something, my response would stick. So our Household Rule was "don't play mom and dad against each other." That, we informed them, was simply bad sportsmanship. Billy and I supported each other even though we disagreed.

One humorous discussion that grew out of our desire to teach our daughters to appreciate differences in others was inviting them to imagine each of us as pieces of fruit. We decided their dad (rough on the exterior but surprisingly delightful on the interior) was a pineapple. Mom (what you see is what you get) was an apple. Alexa (refreshing and funny) was an orange. Ari (tall, golden, and sensitive) was determined - much to her dismay – to be a banana.

As a toddler Ari loved bananas but one day, at the age of four, she opened her lunch box before leaving the house and discovered a bruise on her half piece of banana. Rather than telling me, she began secretly taking her bananas out of her lunch box each day and dropping them behind a cushion on the living room couch before leaving for pre-school. When I finally discovered the collection of two dozen moldy green bananas a few weeks later, I dropped to my knees and praised God for Zip-Lock baggies.

As with Bedroom and household maintenance, Household Rules can be fun. My number one Household Rule, for example, was "I always have time for hugs and kisses." My daughters loved reminding me of this whenever I forgot, they still do.

Property of Self and Others: The one area where my girls can most assuredly improve upon my parenting is in the area of respecting property of others. Not for lack of role modeling, I am entirely awesome at the assignment.

They, however, pretty much follow the "su casa es mi casa" (your home is my home) philosophy when it comes to one another's belongings. Fortunately, with each of them attending college in different cities, things have calmed a bit. In fact now they routinely buy one another clothing as presents. Billy and I look forward to seeing how they teach their children this critical Life Skill they have yet to master.

Transition Times: Transition times refer simply to the moments when any member of a family is transitioning from one major activity or location to another. In the same way stoplights reduce car accidents, respecting Transition Times also reduces emotional collisions.

When our daughters were in grade school, my husband's employment necessitated multiple moves. Although finances were not a non-factor, I'd been "schooled sufficient" on my suitability for super woman status so I temporarily let go of my glorious career goals. We bought a smaller house, drove old cars, and I worked part-time at various odd jobs so I could be home with them during after-school hours.

By the time they reached second and fifth grade, they were fairly independent doing homework and completing after-school projects. So while they focused on schoolwork, I frequently did housework. For some reason, however, just before Billy arrived home each day, I would mysteriously morph into some bizarre form of a human magnet. As if on cue, both girls would exit their bedrooms and run down the hallway requiring my immediate and undivided attention; the house and cell phones would ring in unison; the washing machine would begin to spin out of balance; our automatic pool sweep would spray the living room window, and the news station I was only half-heartedly watching while folding laundry would finally air the one story I'd waited twenty minutes to view.

Since Billy's best friend at the time was Oscar (the affectionate name he gave the pool sweep because it assisted him with managing his territory of pool maintenance) Billy would race outside to rescue him first. Two minutes later, he would re-enter the house and demand to know who tried to choke Oscar to death by dropping a rock in the pool. Of course no one was listening because the girls were now fighting and I was talking on two phones while balancing the washer and complaining about the water stains on the windows.

Suffice to summarize, simple self-preservation mandated modification. The first change I made was to begin calling Billy towards the end of each work day, asking him how things were going and what time he anticipated being home. (I know a simple daily phone call is standard for many couples but Billy and I function highly independently so this was actually a very odd activity for me to commit to on a consistent basis.)

Second, I took care to check in with my daughters reference their overall needs (permission slips, sports applications, etc) prior to Billy arriving home. I also educated the girls on the fact that their father and I needed 15 minutes alone together each day upon his return from the office to catch up with one another before they approached him with their own stories or requests.

Third and most significantly perhaps, I prioritized greeting Billy upon his arrival over everything else. If I was on the phone, I told the person my husband had just arrived home and I would call them back. (My sisters were of course certain my drastic change in behavior meant Billy had started beating me). Instead of having the T.V. on, I put on relaxing music instead.

It is impossible to communicate how dramatically my simple decision to change gears and be wholly present for my spouse for this one quarter-hour of our day improved the overall functioning of our household. Soon I started giving the same focused attention to my daughters during their Transition Times and requesting their respect also during mine. When we succeeded, we restored a surprising amount of dignity and calm to previously high stress times in our daily lives.

Manners: Ok, so your parents taught you not to speak with your mouth full of food but did they also teach you the proper way to position your knife and fork when you are finished? Given the thousands of times your children will greet, dine with, or thank others during their lives, few things are more valuable than educating them about the many ways manners communicate gratitude and respect.

Just like the multiplication tables you assist your children memorizing in second grade, you can review table manners (once learned but since forgotten due to fast food dining) along with them too. Learning manners can be fun when you access information from others passionate about the topic. For very young children, Louise Elderling's book *You've Got Respectful Manners* is a colorful and fun resource. For children age six to ten, Mary O'Donohue's award-winning book *When You Say Thank You Mean It* - with easy to embrace ideas for teaching children soft skills like respect and gratitude - is a treasure chest of wisdom.

Another fun way to enliven the curriculum is to discuss how manners vary between cultures and nations. The internet is a gold mine for these discussions - LinkedIn's International Etiquette groups are particularly interesting.

Finances: Rounding out the category of Respect for Self and Others is the subtopic of finances. If Life Skills were racehorses, finances would give household chores a serious run for the finish when it comes to inspiring conflict. Is it any wonder our financial institutions are crumbling when the hardest assignment teens in developed countries typically complete before leaving home is spending their weekly allowance?

Even the bulk of professionals who call themselves parenting "experts" rarely proactively address the incredibly important topic of teaching children financial skills. With families, schools and professionals all avoiding in-depth education, meltdowns among adults are inevitable.

Fortunately, pioneers like Bill Dwight (Founder of FamZoo) and Sharon Lechter (Co-author of the *Rich Dad Poor Dad* series and Founder of Pay Your Family First) have risen to the challenge and created novel ways to teach children finance skills. Links to theirs and others' Life Skills related Educational Resources are available at http://Parenting2pt0.org.

Lesson #14
Learning multiple ways to communicate respect for self and others is critical to success in the mandatory curriculum.

Chapter Fifteen
Communication & Social Skills

If Personal Care provides the foundation on which Life Skills are developed, Communication and Social Skills serve as the Pillars of the Life Skills Community. The quality of every one of your relationships – even your relationship with yourself - is directly determined by your proficiency in these two critical Life Skills areas. Did you ever receive formal instruction?

<u>Communication</u>

I stated at the outset of this book, and it bears repeating, acquisition of Life Skills is not optional. Free will merely permits you to determine the amount of pain or joy you and others endure until you learn a better way of doing things. Improving your interpersonal communication skills delivers benefits to every avenue of your life – and others'. Below is a brief description of subtopics listed under the category of Communications on the Life Skills Report Card.

Use of "I" Statements: If you have never heard this phrase before you may think I am encouraging people to be self-centered. I am. You and only you have the capacity to listen to your personal GPS. By utilizing "I" statements you own your GPS.

Consider for a moment the following sentence "Robert made Jane weigh 300 pounds." It doesn't sound very logical does it? That's because it isn't. The sentence is in fact physically impossible and, as any linguist will confirm, also semantically incorrect.

Now consider this sentence, "Robert made Jane mad." That sounds better somehow doesn't it? Guess what? It is just as physically impossible and semantically incorrect as the first sentence. Robert may do something but Jane has 100% control over her response, hence the term "response ability." Whether she chooses to listen to her GPS and respond with humor and compassion - or attack back - is entirely up to her.

In the fall of 2011 comedian and talk show host Jimmy Kimmel invited parents to tell their children they ate their Halloween candy and digitally record their response. The videos parents sent in were so numerous and entertaining Kimmel later asked parents to giftwrap something unpleasant for Christmas – like a half-eaten sandwich or rotten banana - then permit their children to open the present early and record their response.

One child screamed and cried hearing his parents ate his Halloween candy, another simply called his mother "sneaky." While children's behavior logically mimics parents, and differences in siblings' responses highlight the role birth order also plays, the diversity of children's responses provides exceptional evidence that there is not one predictable reaction.

Instead of telling your spouse, "You made me mad," and blaming him or her for your choice of response, a more accurate statement is, "I feel really angry right now." This puts the response ability for your emotions where it belongs - with you. It also places the power of effecting change and happiness with you as well.

Proactive/Assertive: The phrase, "An ounce of prevention equals a pound of cure" is true when fighting fires and crime and true in other Life Skills as well. You can be proactive and prepare for challenges, or reactive and complain about things after they happen. The Life Skills Report Card is a proactive instrument for

Life Skills Education. It facilitates communication and goal setting before conflicts arise and enhances likelihood of progress and success. Discussing the concepts of proactive versus reactive communication with your children, and sharing stories of how you too are learning to be more proactive and assertive despite your "advanced" years, will inspire them in their educational journey.

Creativity/Humor: People often think if they disagree with something they must communicate dissatisfaction in an angry tone. That is entirely false. In fact, permitting your tone and tempers to rise typically reduces rather than increases comprehension of whatever you are attempting to communicate.

Marriage ranks right up there on the top of life's most difficult assignments. Disagreements are a predictable part of the process. Fortunately, humor can be as effective as a tongue greeting cotton candy in its ability to dissolve sticky or seemingly intractable conflicts.

Whenever I ask Billy why he does something I think is beneath his (Ph.D., J.D.) intelligence level he closes his eyes, extends both arms out from his sides - palms upward up as if pleading me to comprehend - and replies emphatically "Because I am a man!" No matter how many times he does it, or how aggravated I am with whatever he has done, I always laugh.

If humor was not something you learned growing up, don't despair, you can learn it! In the same manner people learn guitar or piano, you can learn to be funny. Rent videos or attend comedy clubs until you find something humorous. If something makes you laugh, it will likely make someone else laugh as well.

I will insert a word of caution here just in case my husband reads this book. Humor does not mean "telling" others to laugh. If you are telling someone to laugh you are instructing their GPS – telling New York to move. Few things are less funny than comedians who tell their audiences to laugh when they fail to find something funny.

When used appropriately, humor inspires someone to laugh, even in the midst of great difficulty. When you "inspire laughter" you enlighten yourself and others.

Solution Oriented: Have you ever spent hours in a conference room listening to people complain about what isn't working without anyone offering solutions? How did you feel? It is equally frustrating in personal relationships. Encouraging children to offer solutions when they face difficulties - rather than berating them for complaining - will be one of most empowering communication skills you ever teach them and yourself.

Listening/Feedback: One of my favorite jokes addresses the topic of listening. It begins with a man reading his morning paper.

"See sweetheart," he says to his wife seated across from him at the breakfast table. "Here it is in black and white. 'Women use twice as many words a day as men.' "

"Well of course we do," his wife replies. "That is because we have to repeat everything we say."

To which the husband responds, "What?"

The number one complaint of children and parents is that neither is listening. They aren't – but rarely due to lack of desire to communicate. They simply lack knowledge about effective interpersonal communication skills like active listening. Fortunately, multiple books exist on the topic and even beginners will appreciate the improvements the smallest amount of proactive education delivers.

Two parenting books that have - with great justification - remained popular for decades are *Children the Challenge* by Rudolph Dreikurs and *How To Talk so Kids Will Listen and How to Listen So Kids Will Talk* by Adele Faber and Elaine Mazlish. Each provides invaluable recommendations for improving two-way communication with your child.

One chapter in Dreikur's book is titled "Action Not Words." In it he discusses the importance of parents demonstrating value for their own words by saying things only once - then following up with courteous action.

Faber and Mazlich brilliantly provide the most frequently employed parental communication styles with sensitivity and cartoon type illustrations. Billy and I each immediately found our own and much appreciated the dollop of humor that accompanied our dose of humble communication pie.

One part of being a good listener is being honest when you are not in a listening mood. A Buddhist story I once heard tells of a young boy sitting on the edge of a lake at night. When the lake is calm, the boy observes, it reflects the full moon perfectly. When the lake is disturbed, however, the reflection of the full moon is fractured.

What changed in the two scenarios? The moon? No, the moon did not change, the lake changed - the body receiving information and processing it changed. The lake is the listener. When you listen you are also the lake. If you are upset you are not seeing – or hearing – others accurately.

In addition to being aware of when you are not in the right state of mind to listen well, and communicating this candidly to your child, you can also learn techniques for calming your state of mind. Modern child-rearing literature increasingly includes content regarding mindfulness. *Mindful Parent, Happy Child* by Pilar Placone, Ph.D., and *Waking Up* by Raelynn Maloney Ph.D., are two excellent examples.

Listening is not purely the responsibility of the listener; it is also the responsibility of the person speaking. Teens and adults are typically intelligent enough to know not to pour a gallon of milk into an eight-ounce glass, but they fail to make the same calculation when speaking to someone. Are the person's arms folded? Are their eyes pointed elsewhere? Learning to read body language and receptivity is a skill - a skill that improves with education, intention, and practice.

Appropriate Vocabulary: I remember when I was a teenager thinking I would be a "cool" and "accepting" parent when it came to communicating with my own teenagers. Little could I have anticipated of course the severity of the dreaded "Like" affection disorder that struck millions of middle and high school children at the turn of the century.

At first I thought it was just Californian school children who were suffering from a bizarre need to insert the word like in every sentence (and rarely "like" appropriately) but I soon learned teens from other regions of the country and - even internationally – were suffering "like" affection disorder as well.

More than once I challenged my teen daughters to tell me a two-minute story – just two minutes – without inappropriately using the word "like" and they consistently failed to do it. Why? Communication skills are developed over time, with practice and a desire for improvement. When children become teens, friends' opinions and influence increase in importance and parents' opinions wane.

Since my daughters' friends overused the word "like" as much as they did, abandoning it ranked exceedingly low on their Life Skills development list. Fortunately, as they aged, they found themselves in the company of others who frowned upon excessive use of the word "like" and they eventually began to reduce their usage, "like" slightly.

Appropriate vocabulary in one group of people may be considered offensive in another. Educating yourself on customs in various communities and developing the capacity to adjust your vocabulary to maneuver a situation without creating a conversational car crash is a highly valuable – sometimes even lifesaving – skill.

Social Skills

Avoids Being Critical/Focuses On Positives is the first subtopic listed under Social Skills on the Life Skills Report Card and one of the most "critical" when it comes to enjoying positive relations with others – hence its priority placement.

Modern child-rearing literature is keen on advocating encouragement and discouraging compliments and praise. The rationale is that encouragement nurtures children's appreciation for effort and perceptions of self-worth. Praise, by contrast, emphasizes outcome and conditions children to the opinions of others.

I know well the suffering that comes from defining oneself by the effort to please others, so I appreciate the distinction. I also know first-hand, however, the joy that comes from genuinely loving others. Compliments and praise are uniquely powerful in communicating this love and children benefit enormously by learning this fact.

> *"Too often we underestimate the power of a touch, a smile, a kind word, a listening ear, an honest compliment, or the smallest act of caring, all of which have the potential to turn a life around."-Leo Buscaglia*

For fifty-three years I have been told you must love yourself before you can love someone else. This is a lie, a lie that births much misery and discontent. From the day human beings are born they are working on both of their mandatory assignments – learning to love themselves and others. They learn the skills to succeed in these assignments simultaneously - not sequentially.

In fact, the precise opposite is true. Human beings can never fully know themselves – let alone love themselves – until they have *first* experienced unconditional love for another living thing. It may be an animal, it may be a human, but only in loving something outside of yourself do you learn the best about yourself.

> *"When we seek to discover the best in others,*
> *we somehow bring out the best in ourselves."*
> *-William Arthur Ward*

When my daughters were in first and fourth grade they began coming home from school complaining with greater frequency. So one day I challenged them to find an opportunity each day where they could do or say something positive and then share it with me when they came home.

Oh my goodness, I might as well have waived a magic wand! Seemingly overnight our evening family room discussions transformed from miserable to miraculous. Not only did the girls' sense of personal power increase by intentionally seeking an opportunity to make a positive influence in someone else's day, they could not wait to share their stories when they came home.

As mentioned previously, your GPS has its own hardwiring and it favors positives over negatives. Why? Because positives help you and others thrive. Note of caution here. Do not over-value the spoken word. More than ninety percent of what is communicated in your exchanges with others is non-verbal. If you are saying kind words that lack sincerity that is not positive. Conversely, you may tell someone to take a hike (or worse) but if you say it with affection love will be communicated.

This past summer, I assisted my mother as she recovered from double hip replacement in a rehabilitation facility. To be honest, there were probably a hundred things we could have criticized. Instead, we took care to compliment the staff on things done well. In no time at all, nurses were visiting my mothers' room simply to say hello and ask if she needed anything.

The affection was also mutual. The more we expressed genuine compliments, they became more affectionate. The cycle was positively reinforcing. When my mother was discharged from the facility a week later, staff members lined up to hug her goodbye. Happy while she was to be going home, she was genuinely sad to be leaving their loving company.

Takes Ownership in Problems and Conflicts: As one of five girls born in six years, I knew well what parents heard about children's fights was usually little more than the tip of the iceberg. So – challenged while I was when my youngest came sobbing to me because her big "Sissy" had been mean to her - I strived valiantly to mandate my daughters come up with their own solutions to arguments.

Once, when Alexa was five, she decided her solution after a fight with her big sister would be to meditate. So she crossed her legs, closed her eyes, extended her arms with palms turned upwards and chanted, "Ohm, my sister is dumb." They both ended up in stitches, as did I.

How adults resolve conflicts of course provides children live instruction daily. Rather than disparaging adults with low skill levels - and in the process teaching children to be judgmental - adults can use the opportunity to discuss more and less effective ways of communicating. They can teach children to see adults as also learning. *Don't Carve the Turkey with a Chainsaw* by Roger Frame, Ph.D. and *Non-Violent Communication* by Marshall Rosenberg, Ph.D. are two wonderful books for teens and adults to begin improving their conflict resolution skills.

Shoots for Win/Win Outcomes: Children in developed countries are routinely exposed to win/lose philosophy through academia, sports, and board games. Given the difficulties facing our world today, there is possibly not a more critical subcategory on the Life Skills Report Card for positively influencing social dynamics than teaching children skills for achieving win/win outcomes.

I personally advised my children, *"When righteousness and kindness rest in separate palms, choose kindness."* Today, Ari is in her second year of law school. Alexa - an undergraduate majoring in history - plans to follow her "big sis" in her choice of professions. Fortunately, all is not lost.

Absent my prodding, (prayers I confess), Ari was one of just six first year law students to be accepted on her school's Negotiation and Mediation team. In March of 2012, as a second year student, she led her team to first place (out of 46 teams from around the world) at the 2012 International Academy of Dispute Resolution International Mediation Competition (IADR) in Chicago, Illinois. Ari personally ranked second out of more than 138 competitors in individual mediation.

"Win/win" is teachable. Our world will change in miraculous ways when more individuals commit to learning, practicing, and mastering this critical communication skill.

Shares/Altruism: Are you presently volunteering in your community? If not, do you recall a time when you did? Perhaps you coached a little league soccer team or simply helped someone move. How did that feel? Numerous scientific studies have proven that people who volunteer and serve others are not only individually healthier and happier, they also live longer.

Given that human beings are herd mammals - hard wired to know welfare of others is vital to their own survival - the fact that they thrive when caring for others is not terribly surprising. What is surprising is how many people have yet to personally experience the truth of the statement, "It is in giving that we receive."

Have you ever noticed the number of people who succeed individually in business and then begin working even more valiantly for the welfare of others in non-profit forums? Ted Turner, Bill and Melinda Gates, Bono, Warren Buffet and Richard Branson are a few of the more well-known, world changing philanthropists. Fortunately, you do not need to wait until you have millions of dollars before you personally enjoy the benefits of serving others.

When Ari was in fourth grade, she came home one day crying because she'd been unceremoniously kicked out of a (kid's created) recess club called The Pink Ladies. When I asked her, "Why?" she said she didn't know - fellow classmates simply invited her in one day then kicked her out the next. I asked Ari if she really wanted to be part of a club that treated others so insensitively. She replied, "No," but her tone communicated mixed emotions. "Clubs are fun so how about you create one yourself that treats people nicely?" I proposed.

"I can create my own club?" She asked me incredulously. "Absolutely," I responded. Ari's misery transformed to excitement immediately. She and her friend Sarah - who'd also been kicked out of the Pink Ladies Club and had accompanied Ari home that afternoon - sat down to strategize. They came up with the name The Red Heart's Club and decided their purpose would be to spread kindness throughout the community with monthly projects. They also agreed that everyone - boys and girls grade three through six - would be invited to join -everyone except the mean girl that kicked them out of The Pink Ladies Club.

I'd applauded all of their ideas up to this point but – in hearing their goals of excluding someone – I asked them, "If you don't invite her, aren't you treating her just as insensitively as she treated you?

Doesn't that conflict with your goals of kindness?" They reluctantly agreed I had a point.

Knowing something is one thing, experiencing it is something else. In those days I was still learning about the value of secrets to success in the Mandatory Curriculum, so I confess being surprised with just how popular a children's club focused solely on kindness turned out to be. Within just a few weeks The Red Hearts Club had over thirty members - including one whom Ari considered the "coolest" girl in the fifth grade!

For Thanksgiving they orchestrated a canned food drive for the needy. In December, they engaged in old-fashioned door-to-door Christmas caroling and placed toys for the Salvation Army under the town Christmas tree. For Valentine's Day they invited children to bring their blankets and teddy bears to compete in "Best Loved" competitions at the Clayton Library.

At some point members decided the name "Red Hearts Club" was too "girly" and changed their name to the Clayton Community Youth Club (CCYC). For St. Patrick's Day they held a free car wash and paraded up and down Main Street wearing shorts and carrying signs asking, "Do you feel lucky?" (Fortunately social media didn't exist back then or videos condemning us parents as pimps would have gone viral in hours.) Even though the car washes were free, people donated money anyway.

Since they were accepting donations, I educated them about laws governing contributions and registered CCYC as a non-profit organization with the state of California. The children used the funds to rent an inflatable jump tent and create the first ever Kiddie Land area for Clayton's annual summer Art and Wine Festival.

After four years of living in Clayton, Billy took a position with a company in San Diego that necessitated us relocating. CCYC eventually disbanded, but the Kiddy Land section they created at the

Clayton Arts and Wine Festival is operational to this day, growing ever larger and more enchanting.

Enjoys Variety of Activities: I am not a natural athlete, but one thing I do fairly well – thanks to my Canadian parents that loved snow and ice – is snow ski. So, long before my daughters were able to strap on boots and skis, I popped them on snow-capped mountains to play. By the age of seven and eleven, despite living in sunny California, they were both "Mammoth Masters." One day they came to me, however, and said they had bad news.

"What?" I asked.
"Only old people ski" they informed me in unison.
"What?" I asked again, simultaneously wondering if I was the victim of a hidden camera reality show.
"Only old people ski" they confirmed - again in annoying unison,
"What do young people do?" I asked.
"Snowboard."

Having just turned forty, I'd long since accepted that many things I thought were cool and even jazzy – and especially things that were jazzy including the term – were not so cool for my girls. But skiing? How could skiing possibly fall out of fashion - especially when it was the singular thing that made me cool? Fine, I responded, "we will learn to snowboard."

I'd previously heard other adults say "I'm too old for this" but I never pictured myself ever being that person – until my first snowboarding lesson. Thanks to roller blading gear and Mexican coffees, however, pride prevailed and I survived the learning curve.

Trying new things throughout your life is enormously beneficial for your mental, physical, spiritual, and emotional fitness. Having a variety of things you enjoy also creates multiple reservoirs to draw from if the energy you are spending in one area leaves you drained.

Diversity in activities also introduces children to new people and interpersonal challenges. Sadly, the educational opportunity in this area is often undervalued. Whether the conversation during shuttle time is about difficulties with coaches or fellow parents and players, the lesson is always the same. You can teach condemnation of those who are on different levels of learning or compassion for their journey. The mental freeways you assist children in constructing will be ones they travel multiple times throughout their lives, long after the soccer games and piano lessons have ended.

Environmentally Conscious: Imagine for a moment a natural landscape: blue skies, green trees, and pristine waterfalls. What type of emotion does this stir in your body? Now picture the same landscape polluted: skies and water tinged orange, the ground littered with trash. How does that make you feel?

Regardless your perspectives regarding global warming or wildlife preservation, your GPS knows what is essential for survival. It is at peace basking in natural beauty and alarmed when confronted with pollution and decay.

While it is common for parents to not want their child to live in a filthy home, tragically few remember to consider the larger home their children occupy – the planet earth - even fewer effort to abstain from or reduce environmentally harmful activities. Even if recycling and purchasing organic produce was not vogue when you were young, it is never too late to pursue a more conscious path.

Four years ago I decided to switch from using plastic grocery bags to cloth. Suffice to say I proved a highly challenged student. Initially I found myself shopping spontaneously and running into the grocery store for one or two items, then buying several and not having cloth bags. So I decided that if I failed to bring a cloth bag, I would force myself to purchase a new one rather than use plastic. Pretty soon I was donating cloth grocery bags to veterans along with old clothing.

After two years of focusing on how often I failed, and disparaging myself for being challenged with something so easy, I contemplated accepting that utilizing cloth bags when grocery shopping was simply not going to be my contribution to environmental sustainability. No sooner did I think this than my GPS erupted in alarms with the insanity of it.

So I decided instead to be kinder to myself as I worked towards change. Oh my goodness, what an epiphany! Immediately I came up with new methods to facilitate my success. First I stopped buying new cloth bags and instead kept the ones I already had bundled in the trunk of my car.

Second, if I failed to remember to bring cloth bags when I entered the store, or purchased more items than I had bags, I simply placed the grocery items directly into my basket and then put them in cloth bags once I returned to my car. Seemingly overnight, imperfect though I was, I was nevertheless succeeding in my goals. Thank goodness I didn't give up on myself and accept failure!

Have you ever heard the saying "Old age is when a broad mind and a narrow waistband trade places"? Use it or lose it applies. The more new things you do, the more youthful your brain remains. Whatever your age, you can always find something to improve and in the process also increase your mental fitness.

<u>Implementation</u>

Change, regardless how beneficial, is always stressful. So take care to treat the introduction of the Life Skills Report Card to your family with sensitivity. Prepare your children in advance for the fact that you are adopting a new communication tool and why, then introduce the report card when you are rested and relaxed, holiday or summer vacations are particularly good.

Your attitude towards the Life Skills Report Card will shape your child's. If you commit to utilizing it as the valuable communication and character building tool for which it was designed to function, they will appreciate it that way as well.

The Life Skills arena has millions of amazing educators and an even greater number of resources. Unfortunately, with everyone promoting their materials primarily independently, accessing the best possible information as needed in a timely manner can be sufficiently overwhelming to be ignored entirely. Imagine going to the mall and having all the clothes thrown at you, or attending the symphony and having every instrument playing its own song. If Life Skills Educators genuinely care about the publics they serve, as opposed to simply paying their rent or electric bill, they will demonstrate it by unifying and improving their delivery methods. For this reason, in the final section of this book,"The Change" I discuss ways for Life Skills Educators - and everyday citizens - to better harmonize and be the change the world awaits.

Lesson #15
Creating new mental freeways
that run in alignment with your GPS takes time.
Be gentle with yourself as you learn and optimistic of your
eventual success.

Life Skills Report Card Lesson Summary

Lesson #11
If you are not part of the solution,
you are part of the problem.

Lesson #12
Respect personal care for its foundational importance in life.

Lesson #13
Just as you accept teachers teaching children academics,
so too can others be more effective educators of Life Skills.

Lesson #14
Learning multiple ways to communicate respect for others is
critical to success in the mandatory curriculum.

Lesson #15
Creating new mental freeways
that run in alignment with your GPS takes time.
Be gentle with yourself as you learn and optimistic of your
success.

Section Four
The Change

Chapter Sixteen
Andragogy

> *"When people know better*
> *They will do better."*
> *-Maya Angelou*

Two years ago I created a group called Parenting 2.0 (P20) on LinkedIn to nurture discussions between Life Skills educators. Our stated mission is for children's Life Skills Average (LSA) to one day be as appreciated as their Grade Point Average (GPA.)

Anyone who has ever created a profile on LinkedIn knows it is a pretty serious social networking site, with thousands of highly credentialed experts in every possible field. Since my graduate degree is in public administration not human development - and I was advocating something radical by asking that children's LSA (a term I made up) be as appreciated as their GPA - I confess fearing I would attract more insults than members.

Fortunately, the opposite occurred. Our name and mission resonated with others and within 18 months, much to my surprise, we were ranked top of over 200 parenting groups. Today, Parenting 2.0 has over 2000 Life Skills Educators in more than 50 countries as members – many with doctorate degrees in fields related to human development – and it is ranked top of more than 300 parenting groups.

One day someone shared the news that Rick Hanson, a neuropsychologist and author of Buddha's Brain, was going to be in San Diego in February of 2012 for a conference called Bridging the Hearts and Minds of Youth. I loved Rick's books, and had been receiving his electronic newsletter, "Just One Thing" for months, so I wrote him introducing myself as Founder of Parenting 2.0 and asking if he might have time to meet me for coffee.

Given his popularity, I wholly anticipated a polite rejection. Much to my surprise, however, he said yes. So on Saturday, February 4th, 2012 Rick Hanson and I sat down in a quiet corner of the lobby of the Catamaran Hotel and discussed our mutual interest in human development.

It is said that the more you know, the more you know you don't know. Well Rick Hanson knows a lot. He knows for example that knowledge of the human brain has doubled in the past twenty years. He knows recent findings regarding humans' ability to learn new ways of doing things - even into senior years - rival the significance of learning the earth was round not flat.

Despite his vast knowledge, Rick retains a child-like innocence and an absence of ego rare among individuals so learned and well known. Rather than decades of education making him prideful, he is humble and curious, glowing with appreciation of what has yet to be discovered. I found this quality incredibly refreshing and heart-warming. We might just as easily have been two kids sitting on a dock, swinging our legs in the water and marveling at all we did and did not know.

A few days before meeting Rick, I was interviewed via telephone by a woman named Laurie McCabe. Laurie was working on her Ph.D. in Organizational Leadership and interviewing Social Entrepreneurs.

A Social Entrepreneur is someone that recognizes a societal problem and comes up with a novel means of rectifying it. Although the title is relatively new, the role of course has been around for thousands of years.

Like the majority of Social Entrepreneurs, I was one long before somebody informed me of the title. Although I previously described myself as a "Kitchen Sink Activist", today, I use the title Social Entrepreneur in my public profiles. That is how Laurie found me. During the interview, Laurie used the term "andragogy". I have a pretty good vocabulary but I'd never heard that word before and I asked her what it meant. "Adult learning," she answered politely. "Most people use the term pedagogy which means child learning," she continued, "andragogy is far less common." To say I was surprised learning there was a term for something I had been advocating for years is an enormous understatement. It underscored for me the fact that the topic warranted far greater societal attention and discussion.

In saying goodbye to Rick after our meeting, I happened to use the word andragogy, not to impress him - I felt no need for that – but because it simply communicated much quickly. Given his life focus I anticipated that – like Laurie – he would be familiar with the term. Instead, he stopped walking, turned to me and said with delight, "I just learned that word three weeks ago – and I have a pretty good vocabulary!"

Lesson #16
Embrace andragogy,
retain your innocence.

Chapter Seventeen
Billy's Heart

Heart disease runs in Billy's family so when he was 48 I did what many spouses do: I threatened divorce if he did not subject himself to a proper physical. I also told our family doctor that if I was successful getting Billy into his office, he needed to give him a thorough going over because it would be a long time before I could effectively play that hand again.

As usual, Billy's initial tests all proved satisfactory. This time, however, our doctor decided to place him on a treadmill and check his heart under stress. Sure enough, the test revealed an irregularity. So the doctor scheduled a Radioisotope test. This involved injecting Billy's heart with a type of dye and watching it flow through the various chambers. Within minutes, the doctor detected a major blockage and scheduled Billy for surgery.

When I entered Billy's hospital room post-surgery five nurses were staring at an x-ray and talking excitedly. "Is something wrong?" I asked. "Your husband has the most extensive network of collaterals we have ever seen," one of them enthusiastically remarked handing me the x-ray.

Up until this point, I'd only heard the word collateral used as an adjective when referencing unintended damage in warfare, so I was grateful when the nurse continued speaking. "Do you see all these tiny capillaries?" she asked. "They do not normally exist. Your husband's heart grew these to compensate for 100% occlusion (blockage) in his lower anterior descending ventricle. We have never seen a heart with even half as many."

Although I was still not entirely clear what they were saying, I knew they were impressed, so I told them that as his wife of twelve years I took full and total credit for providing just the right amount of additional stress necessary for his heart to achieve the miraculous.

The true Coverwood story of course ran much deeper. In high school, Billy was a basketball player averaging 22 points per game before the three-point era. After joining the college team at Virginia Tech, however, Billy began to experience difficulties breathing. It was rare for young, athletic, and otherwise healthy men to suddenly have heart problems so doctors simply credited the problem to psychosomatic stress caused by his pre-med program and advised him to stop playing.

Thirty years later, Billy's surgeon informed us that he likely suffered an infection in his heart at the age of 18 - an infection that damaged his lower anterior descending ventricle. Although the infection cleared on its own, the ventricle functioned like a rusty drainpipe and began attracting plaque. Eventually, after many years, it closed off entirely.

Most people with Billy's condition simply suffer a heart attack and die. Since Billy continued to remain active in his adult years (playing racquetball, hiking, skiing, and chasing our daughters' rabbits when we brought them in at night) he stimulated his heart just enough for it to gradually grow multiple tiny new pathways. These new growths were sufficient to achieve a twenty percent recovery rate in blood flow. The combination of his prior conditioning, and continued activity, permitted his heart to perform the unfathomable.

The surgeon cleared the blockage by inserting two stints and declared Billy good as new. After coming home, Billy kept remarking how calm he felt. Things that previously caused his heart to pound, and survival hormones to send him into fight or flight response (read hollering as if the world was ending over small stuff), now left him Namaste.

Previously, I'd credited Billy's low tolerance for stress to his upbringing. He was raised the third of four boys in a small coal mining town in Virginia, his father was the town doctor. Their house was on the end of Main Street and his father's practice was in the basement. Consequently, while Billy was a young boy, it was not unusual for him to come home and find some type of trauma: women going into labor, boys with broken arms, or grown men having heart attacks. Learning now the true source of Billy's condition, and how close he'd come to premature death, was enormously humbling.

Human beings have learned a great deal about the variables that shape personalities and physical constitutions. Considerably more, however, remains to be discovered. Until we can construct another human being from scratch in a science lab, it is wise to remain humble when diagnosing or guiding the miraculous.

Lesson #17
Remain humble when diagnosing
or guiding the miraculous.

Chapter Eighteen
Coffee Beans

I work on my computer a great deal and consequently share the same affection for email forwards as most people. Thank goodness I possess greater affection for my friends because it inspires me to read some of their emails anyway. One of the most profound stories I ever read was delivered to me anonymously with the title "Coffee Beans."

One day a teenage girl came home from school, threw her backpack on the kitchen table, and started complaining to her mother about her day. Her mother, standing near the stove, normally permitted her daughter to simply vent. This day, however, she interrupted her.

"Sweetheart," she said as she opened the fridge. "If I put this egg in the boiling water, it will become hard. If I put this carrot in the water, it will become soft. If I put these coffee beans in the water, they will flavor the water. The most important thing you will ever decide is whether to be the egg, the carrot, or the coffee bean."

Lesson #18
The things we resist the most,
the things that deliver us the greatest pain,
often reveal our broader potential.

Chapter Nineteen
Agape

When Alexa was four years old she picked up a puzzle box belonging to her sister. On the cover was a beautiful nature scene with sunshine, glistening waterfalls, colorful foliage, squirrels and deer. Alexa gazed lovingly at the cover then opened the box - clearly hoping to find the same inside. When she saw the irregular, grey, cardboard pieces, her face turned from fascination to dismay. She dumped the contents on the carpet and declared the toy "broken".

Human beings can feel broken, unwanted, unloved. But just like the puzzle, they too simply await the faith of someone committed to reminding them of the masterpiece they are. As with puzzles, the more fractured and complex the pieces, the more impressive the masterpiece once assembled.

> *"The most beautiful people we have known*
> *are those that have known defeat, known suffering,*
> *known struggle, known loss, and have found their way*
> *out of the depths. These persons have an appreciation,*
> *a sensitivity, and an understanding of life that fills them*
> *with compassion, and a deep loving concern."*
> *-Elizabeth Kubler Ross*

Thank goodness no one ever told the redwood tree the proper height for an oak tree. Thank goodness no one ever told the bougainvillea it needed to grow like a tulip. No matter who you are, no matter what your past has been, you are not a mistake. You are a masterpiece, far more powerful than you presently know. Discovering your majesty requires you embrace humility and have faith that your drawing is not yet complete - that something bigger awaits your discovery. It does. If people around you are telling you otherwise, find a better teacher.

The secret is to never stop at feeling broken. Keep going. God does not make junk and you are not the singular exception. Your masterpiece awaits appreciation and dark places await your illumination. In discovering your true self, you will inspire others to discover theirs. In so doing, you will experience the incomparable joy of becoming a Curriculum Scholar.

Lesson #19
Never stop at broken,
dark places await illumination

Chapter Twenty
Occupy or Exemplify?

> *"I believe people are basically good."*
> -Anne Frank

If anyone told me when I created the Life Skills Report Card that it would one day be shared around the world by people with doctorate degrees in child development, and attract sufficient educators to form LinkedIn's top ranked parenting group, I would have been ecstatic. Much to my surprise, however, I ended up feeling precisely the opposite.

The lack of any formal rating or delivery system (as we have with academics) leaves millions of Life Skills educators marketing their information independently and families overwhelmed when searching for valuable information. It is not unlike having oceans of water on one side of a mountain and millions of thirsty people on the other. This fact left me immensely pained.

So I emailed six of our more active members at P20 in the spring of 2010 and asked if they would join me in a conference call to discuss means for bridging the two populations. I confided to everyone that I had no money (in fact I'd recently been laid off), no supporting organization, and I was clueless what to do. I believed, however, that if we could simply begin the process of discussing possible solutions, something would manifest. Much to my delight they each said yes.

One woman was in negotiations with producers in Los Angeles for a television show related to her work, so one of our first ideas was creating a "P20 Talks" show similar to The View.

A second idea was considerably bolder. It involved creation of an online Life Skills University. Our goal with the University was for educators around the world to donate time, information, and resources as a gift to humanity. Everyday people could then access the information freely and provide feedback on resources. The two-way system would then serve as a sort of public rating process. This would enable the University to promote information based not merely on "the best and the brightest" by academic standards, but also the most valuable by human standards.

Around this same time a friend of mine since childhood, Donna Tulip Harris, joined our committee and sent me a photograph of her newly birthed granddaughter Sloan. It was a high definition photo that exquisitely communicated the miracle of creation. Since Sloan represented newness of life and the future, we nicknamed our fictional Life Skills University "Sloan U."

A few weeks later someone told me about an international competition called The Best Brilliant Idea for Humanity. Competition sponsors pledged to feature the top 25 ideas in a book that would be printed and distributed worldwide. Our hopes were that by having the idea of a Life Skills University published in this book, we would attract enough like-minded supporters to launch the University.

The first round of the competition involved public voting. To be truthful, I am typically very humble and was intensely uncomfortable telling others I had submitted an idea in a competition called "The Best Brilliant Idea for Humanity Competition" - let alone ask for their vote. To make matters worse, numerous corporations were shifting their marketing dollars and jumping on social networks. Pepsi was running a campaign called "Pepsi Refresh" that also required public voting and I'd been solicited multiple times. Now here I was contemplating adding to the clamor.

Something kept telling me, however, that so long as I did what I had always done – or found comfortable – nothing substantive would change. So I swallowed my pride and entered our proposal for a Life Skills University in the 2010 Best Brilliant Idea for Humanity competition. We titled our submission "The Life Skills Report Card."

Thankfully, enough of my colleagues, friends and family members voted for The Life Skills Report Card in the first round of the contest to qualify us for the final fifty. The second round required we submit a business proposal. Judges reviewing these selected the 25 ideas to be published in the book.

When I received the news of the final 25 and did not see The Life Skills Report Card included I was crestfallen. At the same time I knew in my heart that the business plan I'd submitted was ...to put it kindly... utopian. Although I did not abandon the idea of the Life Skills University, my sails definitely lost their wind.

Our Parenting 2.0 calls continued but enthusiasm also waned. One morning I was the only one that dialed in. Knowing after twenty minutes it was highly unlikely anyone would be joining me, I decided to stay on the phone anyway - comforted with the fact that at least God was keeping me company. That is when I knew that, despite the lack of a viable plan, I was truly committed to change.

Surprisingly, after thirty minutes, my younger sister Renee Walker dialed in. Renee preceded me in becoming a kitchen sink activist by seven years. Her journey began when she discovered her son's middle school teaching a sex education program that did not comply with state mandated health standards. Shunned by school officials when she pointed out the problem, yet possessing the tenacity of Leigh Anne Touhy (*The Blind Side* fame), Renee kept knocking on bigger doors. Eventually, she founded a group in the San Francisco area called BACHE (Bay Area Community for Health Education). BACHE illuminates the benefits of comprehensive sexuality education and supports schools' compliance with state regulations.

Renee and I had always been close but it was never our goal to collaborate professionally. Her interest in teen safety, however, left her fully aligned with P20's advocacy for a more proactive educational process for Life Skills, so I invited her to join both our group and our planning committee. Renee knew me better than anyone else on the committee but even she was surprised to dial in late and find me on the conference call with myself.

P20 continued its steady growth and, a few weeks later, I happened to post a discussion expressing my appreciation for the strong international family of Life Skills Educators we were attracting. Within a couple of days, dozens of members added their own remarks praising our Parenting 2.0 community. Reading their comments brought tears to my eyes and provided a timely - and much appreciated - injection of optimism.

Several members also expressed interest in organizing a physical gathering for P20 members somewhere on the planet. Although I had a fair amount of experience with event planning, previously I'd always had a budget. Saying yes to organizing a P20 Family Reunion – which essentially equated to an international conference - absent both funds and gainful employment definitely challenged my confidence.

When I thought about it, however, I realized, that all the really critical things I'd ever done in my life were distinguishable only in their lack of certainty: moving to Berlin, Germany alone at the age of 18, getting married, having children, moving to multiple new states, reuniting with my husband after our year-long separation. So I said yes. I did, however, select my current hometown of San Diego, CA for the location.

We titled our conference P20 Talks as a bow to Ted Talks and set a date of August 16th-18th, 2012. Dozens of P20 members volunteered to present. All, including Dr. Rosina McAlpine and Dr. Yvonne Sum from Sydney, Australia, did so without compensation. The goals of the conference mirrored the mission of Parenting 2.0:

1) Recognizing every adult as raising humanity.
2) Highlighting the role of inferior Life Skills in personal and societal problems.
3) Illuminating Life Skills as distinct, critical skill sets.
4) Promoting proactive education by third party educators.
5) Easing parents' access to valuable information and resources.

Around the same time we began planning the P20 Talks conference, a man named Michael Weinberg joined Parenting 2.0. Michael wrote me asking if he could speak to me about a website he was launching called Wizpert. Wizpert functions as a sort of friendly 9-1-1 support service. It utilizes Skype to connect educators and resources for a number of fields, one of them being parenting. Consultants volunteer their time initially. After they receive a certain number of positive ratings, they can begin charging modest fees. Wizpert handles the billing.

In many ways, Wizpert was providing key elements of the services we'd envisioned for our Life Skills University. I was thrilled meeting yet another individual who was as passionate about the value of better connecting educators and the public as me. I also found Michael's commitment to keeping the initial level of consulting free spiritually refreshing. Consequently, I was more than happy to support him and his partner Stefan D'Heedene in their launch.

I even signed on as a consultant and added their "Call a Wizpert" button to my Life Skills Report Card website.

During this same time period, the world was rocking with its own labor pains. News of "the Arab Spring", "Financial Collapse", and the "Occupy Movement," dominated headlines daily. Time Magazine even named "The Protestor" their Person of The Year for 2011.

Seeing everyday people effecting massive change was inspiring. Multiple P20 members began expressing confidence in our ability to nurture more substantive change through expanded forums. New York based Dr. Yolanda Wattsjohnson proposed forming Parenting 2.0 groups in various cities to expand our impact. Melissa Pazen in Chicago, Illinois, and Karen Shaw in Manchester, UK, organized P20 meetings in their respective regions.

These small steps planted the seed for unveiling plans for an international volunteer organization called The Global Presence at our August P20 Talks Conference. The Global Presence has three primary humanitarian service goals:

1.) Creation of a professional Guild to unify Life Skills Educators.

2.) Creation of an objective third party rating system for critical resources (Like Givewell for non-profits.)

3.) Creation of volunteer staffed Global Presence Educational Centers around the world. These Educational Centers will honor parents for their service on the front lines raising humanity and facilitate access to critical resources.

In contemplating The Global Presence, I knew that it was already functioning informally. Loving, kind, peace-oriented people were helping one another in ways large and small daily, offering encouragement and wisdom for relationship challenges and childrearing. We would simply be amplifying the process by formally unifying educators and giving volunteers a platform through which to be appreciated and supported in their service.

A man named Larry Wilcox, who had extensive acting and production experience in Los Angeles, joined Parenting 2.0 in the summer of 2011 while conducting research for a documentary about teens at risk. Larry was uniquely pre-attuned to our goals and offered to produce the P20 Talks conference and assist in formation of The Global Presence.

Another tenacious Parenting 2.0 member, a Word Press expert named Gloria Antonelli who I'd worked with on some minor projects, offered to help us construct a Parenting 2.0 website free of charge. Gloria even flew from Chicago to San Diego one week in December 2011 to meet with me personally and discuss design.

Although we knew we would eventually need a separate and more dynamic website for The Global Presence, particularly if it was going to support the diversity of international communities we envisioned blossoming, we decided to include information about it on the Parenting 2.0 site anyway. That week I drafted The Global Presence Pledge:

The Global Presence Pledge

I pledge to be the change I wish to see in the world.

I pledge to celebrate diversity and foster community.

I pledge to think globally and serve locally.

I pledge to nurture peace in homes and between nations.

I pledge patience and optimism with myself and others as we learn to thrive individually and commune optimally.

I pledge to own my role in raising humanity.

I pledge to respect the fragility and dignity of my planetary home.

I pledge to honor the divine wisdom of myself and others.

I pledge to support The Global Presence Community in thought, word and deed.

I pledge humility in my role as a member of The Global Presence.

I pledge gratitude for the opportunity to link arms with others in service to humanity.

Anyone age 18 or older can go to http://parenting2pt0.org/ the-global-presence take the pledge and be recognized as nurturing a new, more compassionate, and caring era of humanity. Service opportunities range from simply signing The Global Presence Pledge, featuring The Global Presence membership badge on electronic profiles, to community service.

Community volunteers help bridge the gap between educators and parents by providing a physical staff of humble, kind-hearted individuals, committed to supporting parents as they raise future generations. Picture the town hall or community center serving hugs, tea, and biscuits and providing personal research assistants to access information while you visit with people that value your service on the front line raising humanity.

Global Presence Educational Centers can be created from scratch by everyday individuals confident of their value and optimistic about their personal capacity to effect positive change. Alternately, they can be formed within existing organizations like childcare centers, community service organizations, Mommy and Me groups, corporations, and even prisons – any place where people are willing to gather to improve lives of others.

> *"Man's capacities have never been measured;*
> *nor are we to judge of what he can do by any*
> *precedents, so little has been tried."*
> *-Henry David Thoreau*

I would like to end "Kissing the Mirror" by telling you that, thanks to basically good people everywhere heeding the call to unify, The Global Presence became the world's largest volunteer organization. I would like to describe how societal problems were alleviated when people committed to life-long learning.

I would like to say adults everywhere became more conscious and proactive in their role of raising humanity and no other young mother ever felt so inferior as to attempt suicide.

That part of this story, however, has yet to transpire. That part of this story will be written by you. I will tell you in closing I know you exist. I know you are already supporting one another in times of need in ways large and small.

I know the numbers of people nurturing love and peace on the planet outnumber those who believe war is our best answer. I believe passionately that by giving you a formal forum such as The Global Presence to unify, and supporting you in your efforts, the results of your labors will be exponentially magnified.

> *"Alone we can do so little; together*
> *we can do so much."*
> *-Helen Keller*

The Change the world awaits is here. Please own your role by signing the Global Presence Pledge today then kissing your mirror! I look forward in complete sincerity and confidence to the year when Time Magazine nominates you, The Exemplifier, their Person of the Year.

Lesson #20
The change the world awaits is here!
Kiss your mirror!

The Change Lesson Summary

Lesson #16
Embrace andragogy,
retain your innocence.

Lesson #17
Remain humble when diagnosing
or guiding the miraculous.

Lesson #18
The things we resist most,
the things that deliver us the greatest pain,
often reveal our broader potential.

Lesson #19
Never stop at broken,
dark places await illumination

Lesson #20
The Change the world awaits is here!
Kiss your mirror!

Appendix A
The Paradigm Shift of Parenting 2.0

Old: Those with children in their homes are raising children.
New: Every adult has a role raising humanity.

Old: Life Skills Education resembles genetic inheritance.
New: Life Skills Education resembles academics.

Old: Life Skills are important for surviving.
New: Life Skills are critical to thriving.

Old: Children learn what they live.
New: Children learn what adults and others take time to teach them and what they elect to learn themselves.

Old: Value Perfection.
New: Value Imperfection.

Old: Formal education ends in early adulthood.
New: Education is a life-long process.

Old: Human beings are hard wired to dominate.
New: Human beings are hard wired to cooperate.

Old: Failure is to be discouraged.
New: Failure is evidence you are trying something new.

Old: Children and adults can be broken.
New: Children and adults can be dispirited, they can also be inspired.

Old: Education in Interpersonal Communication is called Therapy.
New: Education in interpersonal communication is called education in interpersonal communication.

Old: Learning Life Skills is about discipline.
New: Learning Life Skills is fun and inspiring.

Old: Embrace Experts when nurturing humanity.
New: Embrace Humility when nurturing humanity.

Old: Value conformity
New: Celebrate diversity

Old: Value Independence.
New: Value Interdependence.

Old: You must love yourself before you can love others
New: You cannot know your true self until you unconditionally love others.

Old: Serve self
New: Serve others

The Mandatory Curriculum Lesson Summary

Lesson #1
Every human being faces the same mandatory curriculum -
surviving and communing with others.

Lesson #2
The high bar for performance in The Mandatory Curriculum is
thriving personally and helping others to thrive equally.

Lesson #3
Life is like an Olympic Torch Run with each generation,
each individual,
facing their own unique terrain and challenges.

Lesson #4
Your human GPS is your personal compass for thriving
and supporting others in thriving also.

Lessons #5
Free will does not mean you choose the assignments. It merely
permits you to choose the amount of pain you and others
endure until you learn what is necessary to thrive and commune
optimally with others.

Algebra and Apples Lesson Summary

Lesson #6
Personal perception is necessarily
subjective and limited.
Retire being "right," respect perspectives of others.

Lesson #7
Those who fail learn humility and compassion -
essential skills for becoming a Curriculum Scholar.

Lesson #8
Like academics, Life Skills benefit from
proactive education and a dynamic curriculum.

Lesson #9
The harder the task,
the greater the value of instruction from qualified educators,
at any point in life.

Lesson #10
You can walk away from a person
but you cannot walk away from the assignment.

Life Skills Report Card Lesson Summary

Lesson #11
If you are not part of the solution,
you are part of the problem.

Lesson #12
Respect personal care for its foundational importance in life.

Lesson #13
Just as you accept teachers teaching children academics,
so too can others be more effective educators of Life Skills.

Lesson #14
Learning multiple ways to communicate respect for others is
critical to success in the mandatory curriculum.

Lesson #15
Creating new mental freeways
that run in alignment with your GPS takes time.
Be gentle with yourself as you learn and optimistic of your success.

The Change Lesson Summary

Lesson #16
Embrace andragogy,
retain your innocence.

Lesson #17
Remain humble when diagnosing
or guiding the miraculous.

Lesson #18
The things we resist most,
the things that deliver us the greatest pain,
often reveal our broader potential.

Lesson #19
Never stop at broken,
dark places await illumination

Lesson #20
The Change the world awaits is here!
Kiss your mirror!